THE
Song
OF
Redeeming
Love

THE

Song
OF
Redeeming
Love

SPENCER J. CONDIE

DESERET BOOK

SALT LAKE CITY, UTAH

Library of Congress Cataloging-in-Publication Data

Condie, Spencer J.
  The song of redeeming love / Spencer J. Condie.
    p.   cm.
  Includes bibliographical references and index.
  ISBN 1-57008-771-7 (alk. paper)
  1. Spiritual life—Church of Jesus Christ of Latter-day Saints.   I. Title.
  BX8656 .C553 2002
  248.4'89332—dc21   2001006459

Printed in the United States of America   21239-6915
Edwards Brothers, Inc., Ann Arbor, MI

10   9   8   7   6   5   4   3   2   1

*To Dorothea
who knows the song
and sings it well*

If ye have experienced a change of heart, and if ye have felt to sing the song of redeeming love, I would ask, can ye feel so now? (Alma 5:26).

Contents

Acknowledgments

It is difficult to properly express my gratitude to numerous friends who have been so helpful in bringing this book to fruition without implicating them in its deficiencies. I am grateful for the enthusiastic encouragement of Sheri Dew in the embryonic stages of the manuscript. I give generous thanks to Cory Maxwell, Janet G. Lee, Virginia H. Pearce, and Robert L. Millet for helpful suggestions that strengthened the book. And I appreciate very much the candid comments of Stefanie Condie, who loves me enough to tell me the truth.

I express sincere gratitude to Kathleen Moultrie, who so competently, cheerfully, and creatively transformed chaos into a manuscript approaching coherence. Michael Morris at Deseret Book also deserves my appreciation for his conscientious editorial comments and suggestions.

I am especially grateful for the Brethren with whom I am blessed to labor and for their example and perpetual influence for good in my life and in the lives of my family members.

Introduction

And I did read many things unto them which were written in the books of Moses; but that I might more fully persuade them to believe in the Lord their Redeemer I did read unto them that which was written by the prophet Isaiah; for I did liken all scriptures unto us, that it might be for our profit and learning (1 Nephi 19:23).

When the winds of weakness beat against our souls and against the souls of our loved ones, we gain a measure of solace in the apostle Paul's declaration that "all have sinned, and come short of the glory of God" (Romans 3:23). In our introspective moments, we receive sporadic spiritual nudges to make changes in our lives, like spending less time on the golf course so we can spend more time with the family, or selling some of our recreational "toys" so we can be more faithful in observing the Sabbath, or downsizing our home so we can reduce the mortgage and increase our service.

Ofttimes we must *hollow* our lives before the Lord can *hallow* them. Sometimes hollowing occurs at the individual level; other times it occurs at the collective level. Such was the case when Alma served as both the political and spiritual leader of the Nephites. His spiritual labors bore great fruit as "about

1

three thousand five hundred souls" were converted and baptized and "united themselves to the church" (Alma 4:5). Unfortunately, this rapid growth was not sustained because the members of the Church failed to live the commandments of God (Alma 4:10). This ecclesiastical challenge caused Alma to relinquish his political position as chief judge to spend his entire time preaching the gospel, "seeing no way that he might reclaim them save it were in bearing down in pure testimony against them" (Alma 4:19).

His first stop was in the land of Zarahemla, where he posed forty-two soul-searching questions to those who were evidently wavering in their faith. These questions included such queries as these: "Have ye walked, keeping yourselves blameless before God?" "Are ye stripped of pride?" "Is there one among you who is not stripped of envy?" (Alma 5:27–29). Alma did not simply ask the people if they were humble and free from covetous inclinations; he asked if they had *stripped* themselves of pride and envy. In accepting the gospel during the dispensation of the fulness of times, we must truly lose ourselves (Matthew 10:39), deny ourselves of all ungodliness (Moroni 10:32), cleanse the inner vessel (Alma 60:23), and give away all our sins (Alma 22:18), for the *emptiness* precedes the *fulness*.

The seeds of the restoration of the fulness of the gospel sprang from the emptiness of a fourteen-year-old boy who sensed that he lacked wisdom. Ever since Gutenberg had begun printing the Bible in large quantities in the mid-fifteenth century, millions of people had read James' epistle, but it was Joseph Smith who humbly recognized that he really did lack wisdom. Thus, he followed James' prescription for the problem (James 1:5). He asked of God, and because he came to God empty, he was prepared to be filled.

Alma reminded the inhabitants of Zarahemla of his father's missionary labors wherein he baptized many in the waters of

Mormon. Alma said the souls of those early converts "did expand, and they did sing redeeming love" (Alma 5:4–9). He then asked the people of Zarahemla, "Have ye spiritually been born of God? Have ye received his image in your countenances? Have ye experienced this mighty change in your hearts? . . . If ye have experienced a change of heart, and if ye have felt to sing the song of redeeming love, I would ask, can ye feel so now?" (Alma 5:14, 26).

In Ammon's missionary homecoming address, he reported on the thousands of Lamanites who had been "loosed from the pains of hell" and were "brought to sing redeeming love" (Alma 26:13).

A review of the teachings of Book of Mormon prophets shows clearly that the song of redeeming love is intended not only to be *their* song but also *our* song. It is the song of the mother who moistens her pillow with tears for an errant child. It is the song of a man or woman who finally escapes from the snares of addiction and rediscovers the great gift of moral agency. It is the song of worried parents who one day gratefully realize that their children did not turn out so badly after all. It is the song of children grown older who love and forgive their imperfect parents. It is the song of each of us as we feel the Father's love in sending His Son as a ransom for our sins but who requires us to sacrifice those sins in order to know Him and His Son. We must come to the Father and the Son empty in order to receive the fulness.

Pursuant to Nephi's counsel, I have made a humble attempt to "liken all scriptures unto us" (1 Nephi 19:23) by using various vignettes from the lives of individuals like you and me and like Alma and his wayward associates who learned to sing the song of redeeming love.

ONE

Lehi's Song of Redemption

Adam fell that men might be; and men are, that they might have joy. And the Messiah cometh in the fulness of time, that he may redeem the children of men from the fall. And because that they are redeemed from the fall they have become free forever, knowing good from evil; to act for themselves and not to be acted upon, save it be by the punishment of the law at the great and last day, according to the commandments which God hath given (2 Nephi 2:25–26).

A dozen years ago I accepted the assignment to interview an elderly sister who had been excommunicated from the Church many years previously. More than a year after her rebaptism, her bishop and stake president had recommended her to the First Presidency as one worthy to have her temple blessings restored. I telephoned her to make an appointment for an interview and informed her that I would be visiting her stake in about two months and would be pleased to meet her at that time.

With a tinge of indignation, she replied, "Brother Condie, I am in my mid-eighties. I may not be around in two months! If you are going to be in your office tomorrow, I will catch the train and be there tomorrow at 4 P.M."

Of course, I readily agreed to her recommendation. The

next day, right on the dot at 4 P.M., this lovely, radiant, elderly sister came huffing and puffing into my office. After allowing her time to catch her breath, I began our interview. About twenty-five years previously, her husband had fallen critically ill and become an invalid. He was a rather large man and she was a rather frail woman, so caring for him became an arduous burden for her. She had an extremely difficult time changing his bedsheets and helping him into and out of the bathtub, but to her good fortune, a strong, kindly neighbor came to her assistance. This Good Samaritan was at her beck and call, standing ever ready to help in any way possible.

As the weeks and months progressed, her husband's condition worsening and her need for help increasing, this lovely sister's admiration for her compassionate neighbor grew. One day, in an unguarded moment, they expressed inappropriate affection for each other. As a result, she lost her membership in the Church and her temple blessings, including the right to wear the sacred, protective temple garment. For nearly twenty years she received absolutely no contact from other Church members, accepting this lack of association as the normal punishment for her sins.

With tear-brimmed eyes, she recounted how two "young men" (probably in their forties) had knocked on her door three years before, introducing themselves as her home teachers. She said, "I was so surprised and overjoyed to see them!" They explained that they had come to her home to invite her back to Church. They provided transportation to all meetings and assured her that she was welcome among a community of Saints that had truly missed associating with her. With the passage of several months she demonstrated to her priesthood leaders that she had, indeed, brought forth the fruits of repentance. Another disciplinary council was held, a court of love, and the bishopric felt the spiritual confirmation that she should be rebaptized.

Seldom have I had the blessing of interviewing someone who was so pure, so humble, and so completely without guile. Authorized by the First Presidency and the president of the Quorum of the Twelve, I restored unto her all she had lost: her endowment and sealing to her husband, the privilege of wearing the sacred temple garment, and the right to enter the holy temple.

At the conclusion of the blessing, I counseled her to prepare to return to the temple the next time the members of her ward and stake visited the temple together. Again, with some impatience, she said, "You keep forgetting that I'm in my mid-eighties. I might not be around for the next stake temple day. I need to go to the temple tomorrow before returning home on the train." The next morning she went to the house of the Lord, where she spent most of the day. The hollowing had occurred during a quarter of a century and now she was ready for the hallowing. As she returned home, she sang, as it were, the song of the Savior's redeeming love.

THE LORD'S SONG

After centuries of successive prophetic warnings to repent, the Hebrew children of the southern kingdom of Judah were taken into Babylonian captivity around 587 B.C. The psalmist eloquently captured the poignancy of their pathetic plight:

> *By the rivers of Babylon,*
> *There we sat down,*
> *Yea, we wept, when we remembered Zion.*
> *We hanged our harps upon the willows*
> *In the midst thereof.*
> *For there they that carried us away captive*
> *Required of us a song;*

And they that wasted us required of us mirth, saying,
Sing us one of the songs of Zion.
How shall we sing the Lord's song in a strange land?
(Psalm 137:1–4)

Many people who have strayed from the Church can resonate with that yearning to sing the Lord's song but have faced that same desperate question: How can I sing the Lord's song in strange surroundings? It is impossible to sing the Lord's song in a place where Satan's clamor muffles the melody and lyrics of the Lord's song. It is impossible in a tattoo parlor where one's body temple is being desecrated. It is impossible in a bar, where drinking alcohol diminishes moral reasoning. It is impossible while viewing pornography in any of its multifarious forms. And it is impossible amid the blare of quarrelsome voices in a home filled with contention.

It is much easier to softly sing the Lord's song while on our knees in our private chamber in the attitude of prayer or during family home evening when we are encircled by the riches of eternity. The perfect place to learn the lyrics of the Lord's song is in His holy house. There, in the sanctity and silence of the celestial room, we can sing the Lord's song as someone who is homeward bound, no more held captive in a strange land.

Elderly Lehi, near the end of his life, testified to his family, "The Lord hath redeemed my soul from hell; I have beheld his glory, and I am encircled about eternally in the arms of his love." Continuing, he said, "And now that my soul might have joy in you, and that my heart might leave this world with gladness because of you . . . awake, my sons; put on the armor of righteousness" (2 Nephi 1:15, 21, 23). These words to his two oldest sons did not fall on particularly receptive ears; however, Jacob absorbed his father's teachings of Christ's redemption so well that he perpetuated them throughout his own ministry.

Lehi tenderly reminded Jacob, "I know that thou art

redeemed, because of the righteousness of thy Redeemer; for thou hast beheld that in the fulness of time he cometh to bring salvation unto men. And thou hast beheld in thy youth his glory" (2 Nephi 2:3–4).

Lehi testified: "Redemption cometh in and through the Holy Messiah; for he is full of grace and truth. Behold, he offereth himself a sacrifice for sin, to answer the ends of the law, unto all those who have a broken heart and a contrite spirit; and unto none else can the ends of the law be answered.

" . . . There is no flesh that can dwell in the presence of God, save it be through the merits, and mercy, and grace of the Holy Messiah, who layeth down his life according to the flesh, and taketh it again by the power of the Spirit, that he may bring to pass the resurrection of the dead, being the first that should rise.

"Wherefore, he is the firstfruits unto God, inasmuch as he shall make intercession for all the children of men; and they that believe in him shall be saved.

"And because of the intercession for all, all men come unto God; wherefore, they stand in the presence of him, to be judged of him according to the truth and holiness which is in him. Wherefore, the ends of the law which the Holy One hath given, unto the inflicting of the punishment which is affixed, which punishment that is affixed is in opposition to that of the happiness which is affixed, to answer the ends of the atonement" (2 Nephi 2:6–10).

Lehi discussed the Atonement within the larger context of the great plan of happiness, the plan of salvation, beginning with Adam and Eve, explaining that "if Adam had not transgressed he would not have fallen, but he would have remained in the garden of Eden. . . . And [Adam and Eve] would have had no children; wherefore they would have remained in a state of innocence, having no joy, for they knew no misery;

doing no good, for they knew no sin. . . . Adam fell that men might be; and men are, that they might have joy" (2 Nephi 2:22–23, 25).

This is one of the central messages of the Book of Mormon and of the restored gospel of Jesus Christ. While it is true that it "must needs be, that there is an opposition in all things" (2 Nephi 2:11) in order to allow us to optimally use our moral agency and freedom of choice, only the right choices lead to joy (2 Nephi 2:11). We did not come to earth merely to suffer but to serve, and through losing ourselves in the service of others we become partakers of joy. While it is true that our mortal existence requires sacrifice, in nearly every instance sacrifice involves giving up something good for something even better. Sacrifice is the hollowing in preparation for the hallowing of service and the reaping of blessings that come to us when we lose ourselves in service to others.

Lehi left his family with the prophetic testimony that "the Messiah cometh in the fulness of time, that he may redeem the children of men from the fall. And because that they are redeemed from the fall they have become free forever, knowing good from evil; to act for themselves and not to be acted upon, save it be by the punishment of the law at the great and last day, according to the commandments which God hath given" (2 Nephi 2:26). Then, sensing that his life was drawing to a close, this venerable prophet once again admonished his sons: "I would that ye should look to the great Mediator, and hearken unto his great commandments; and be faithful unto his words, and choose eternal life, according to the will of his Holy Spirit" (2 Nephi 2:28).

When Martin Harris lost the first 116 pages of the newly translated manuscript of the Book of Mormon, the Prophet Joseph Smith was heartsick because those pages contained the writings of father Lehi. But the Lord, foreseeing the end from the beginning, and sensitive to the foibles of His spiritual off-spring, provided a backup plan. Nephi recorded large portions of his father's visions, dreams, prophecies, teachings, and counsel, adding them to his own record. Nephi refers to "my father" more than three dozen times within the first ten chapters of 1 Nephi. Lehi's record may be incomplete, but Nephi's abridgement is pithy and profound, especially as he records his father's song of redeeming love.

SIN SHALL BE FORGIVEN

In the Gospel of Matthew, the Lord provides a panoramic glimpse of the meaning of the infinite Atonement: "All manner of sin and blasphemy shall be forgiven unto men *who receive me and repent*; but the blasphemy against the Holy Ghost, it shall not be forgiven unto men" (JST, Matthew 12:26; emphasis added).

On February 26, 2001, an unusual press conference was held simultaneously in New York City, Los Angeles, Oakland, Chicago, and Washington, D.C. These diverse venues were all linked by satellite to the originating location at the Family History Library in Salt Lake City. The Church called these conferences to officially announce the completion of the extraction and indexing of the Freedman Bank's records.

At the conclusion of the Civil War, the United States government organized the Freedman's Bureau to help recently freed African-American slaves find employment and housing and adjust to their newly won status in a free society. The Freedman Bank, in which approximately 480,000 African-Americans invested their hard-gained earnings, was an adjunct to this agency.

Unfortunately, through mismanagement and fraudulent activities among some of the bank directors, the Freedman Bank became insolvent and most of its clients lost their meager savings. Notwithstanding this personal tragedy to so many honest, hardworking bank customers, the Freedman Bank's records have become a blessing to as many as eleven million modern-day African-Americans.

A dozen years ago, Marianne Taylor of the Family and Church History Department brought to the awareness of Church leaders the fact that the National Archives held microfilm copies of the records of Freedman Bank customers. These records would need to be extracted and systematically indexed for ready accessibility, but Sister Taylor foresaw a virtual gold mine for African-Americans wishing to trace their ancestry. She contacted Darius 'Gray, a prominent Black member of the Church in Salt Lake City, to discuss how the massive extraction efforts could begin. Eleven years ago, an invitation was extended to inmates of the Utah State Prison to voluntarily participate in extracting, recording, cataloging, and indexing the records. During the extraction work, more than five hundred inmates participated in the program.

On March 16, 2001, a meeting was convened in the prison chapel honoring the fifty inmates still in prison who had completed the Freedman Bank project. The inmate leader gave a very moving talk describing his involvement with the project. He revealed that many times tears rolled down his cheeks as he read of the harsh treatment of these African-Americans. Accounts of their abuse reawakened his remorse for the physical pain and emotional anguish he had caused the victims of his crimes. He choked back the tears as he expressed his gratitude for the opportunity of being involved in this family history work.

Following our meeting, I complimented the inmate on his heartfelt remarks. A few days later he sent me a lengthy letter rehearsing his conversion experience. With his permission, I share some of the highlights of his pain and suffering and ultimate joy in experiencing a mighty change of heart:

"After twelve years of a life filled with drugs and crime, I came to a realization of my spiritual status before my Maker. Although this awareness of my spiritual demise was triggered by the law, I made the decision to repent and rediscover my God and religious beliefs.

"The first few years into my repentance process, I read the Book of Mormon over and over. I felt with each reading a greater desire and concern for the welfare and happiness of the people I had victimized over the years.

"For the next seven years, I prayed for my victims. I prayed that they might receive the strength to forgive me, knowing that the ability to forgive would help the healing process in them. I also continued praying to the Lord that He would allow me to feel their pain.

"Over the years I continued to pray for my repentance and my victims. I attended all of my church meetings and worked on my genealogy.

"In June of 1994, I awoke one morning with some feelings of anxiety, hopelessness, anguish, and despair. These emotional feelings stayed with me throughout the day and increased over the next few weeks. By the end of June, my emotional state was such that I was not sleeping well. I also started a morning ritual of vomiting. In mid-July, my anguish, anxiety, and mental condition reached the point that I was only sleeping one hour out of twenty-four, and then only from exhaustion. The physical sensations in my body became so intense that I describe them as a fire burning inside my body. I was only eating one meal a day and doing nothing more than staying in bed trying to endure the pain.

"Nights were filled with trembling to the point of sweating until my bed was completely soaked. As my physical condition weakened, the symptoms grew more and more intense. By August, I was seeking medical help, which subjected me to different types of drugs used in treating depression and anxiety. I received no relief from the medication; my anguish, hopelessness, and fire only increased with each passing day.

"I was visited by my bishop, and after talking with him for a few hours it was decided that we would fast and pray along with his counselors, family members, and some friends. We also decided that after we had prepared ourselves, he would give me a blessing of healing the following Sunday.

"At the beginning of my blessing, my bishop started to cry and told me that he could not give me a blessing of healing at that time. But during my blessing, he told me that the Lord wanted me to go through this experience because of the future mission I had to do in my life. He told me that the Lord wanted to see what kind of timber I was made of. He also told me that when the pain became extremely bad, I was to call upon the Savior and He would come to me and give me some relief.

"After this blessing, I felt some hope and power. I had a desire to stand up and prove to God that I do have what it takes, and I am strong enough to endure His blessings. As I started fighting back, proving my strength, the pain increased to the point that the people around me admitted me to the hospital. . . .

"I remembered the blessing that my bishop gave me, telling me that when the pain got to the point that I could not bear it, to call upon Christ and He would come to me. I knelt down and prayed, telling Him that I had no idea what was happening to me and that I needed Him to come to me and help me. I told Him that I was too weak and that if it was His will, to please take my life. I told Him that I could no longer endure what was taking place in me.

"As I was praying, I felt someone's arms around me. I thought that it was the guard on nightshift at first, but there was no one there. I felt a warmth and love come over me, and I was laid down upon the bed. The pain was gone and I fell asleep. I awoke six hours later, the longest sleep I had received for months. I felt okay and prayed to the Lord, thanking Him for the relief and love He gave me. I then told Him that I was ready to receive His will for me, after which the pain and anguish immediately returned.

"When the doctor came to see me, I related to him my thoughts of wanting to kill myself or someone else. He told me that this particular medication in some patients did have that side effect. After some other tests, the doctor told me that I was dying and that he had never seen a case of anxiety so severe. He told me that if I could not pull out of it soon, I would be dead in a month. He said that because of my long-term drug addiction, my chemical makeup made it difficult for him to treat me.

"I implored blessings from other priesthood leaders, the latter of which, among other things, said, 'I bless you that you must face this trial, and it is the desire of our Lord that you must pass through the refiner's fire like those before you. You must understand the things that you will learn and need from this blessing. Have faith and endure. The Lord is very aware of your pain and suffering.'

"He also told me the same thing my bishop told me in my first blessing, that 'when the pain becomes so bad, pray and call upon Christ, and He will come to you.'

"I thought of my Savior and what He went through in the garden. I know that I was only feeling a portion of my sins. However, that portion of my sins administered by God would have killed me if I had had to feel all of them at once.

"From my experience, I can comprehend how a person could bleed from every pore. What amazes me most is that the Savior did not die. I know that my small payment for my sins would have killed me if I had been allowed to pay for them all at once. Only a God could have escaped with only bleeding from every pore.

"I am blessed that the Lord would think that I was worthy of being able to experience a portion of what my Savior suffered in the garden. I am blessed to feel the pain that I caused my victims. I am blessed to feel the unquenchable fire of anguish and brimstone. I am blessed to realize that I am nothing and that the consequences of sin could totally dissolve my physical being into dust. I am blessed to feel hell.

"Today I am still struggling with my anguish and hell. However, the Lord has allowed me only small daily portions, just enough to hate sin and to love my Savior for what He suffered for me. It has been six years since this experience, and I am one of the most blessed men on the earth.

"I leave you my testimony that wickedness never was happiness, and that Alma the Younger knew what it meant to have one's soul harrowed up by sin."

President Boyd K. Packer has declared, "Save for those few who defect to perdition after having known a fulness, there is no habit, no addiction, no rebellion, no transgression, no offense exempted from the promise of complete forgiveness."[1]

How can we sing the Lord's song in a strange land? Certainly, prison walls built to contain and restrain the so-called worst of our society constitute a strange land set apart from the rest of the law-abiding citizenry. But to paraphrase the poet, iron bars do not a prison make. For those who come to know and feel the cleansing power of the Atonement in their lives, though their sins may have been as scarlet, even in a dark prison cell they can sing one more strain of praise for the Lord's redeeming love.

NOTE

1. Packer, "The Brilliant Morning of Forgiveness," *Ensign*, November 1995, 19.

TWO

Nephi's Song of Loving-Kindness

And the world, because of their iniquity, shall judge him to be a thing of naught; wherefore they scourge him, and he suffereth it; and they smite him, and he suffereth it. Yea, they spit upon him, and he suffereth it, because of his loving-kindness and his long-suffering towards the children of men (1 Nephi 19:9).

The first chapter of the Book of Mormon describes Lehi's vision in which he sees the Savior followed by the Twelve as they minister upon the earth. Lehi was presented with a book to read, and "as he read he was filled with the Spirit of the Lord" (1 Nephi 1:12). We, like Lehi, can enjoy the Spirit of the Lord as we search the scriptures. Nephi later included a detailed description of his father's dream of the path leading to the tree of life: "And it came to pass that I beheld that the rod of iron, which my father had seen, was the word of God, which led to the fountain of living waters, or to the tree of life; which waters are a representation of the love of God; and I also beheld that the tree of life was a representation of the love of God" (1 Nephi 11:25).

The fountain of living waters is a recurrent symbol throughout holy writ, and considering the arid geographical seedbed from which much scripture has sprung, water's life-sustaining property gains immediate access to the reader's imagination. When the Savior spoke to the Samaritan woman at the well, she may not have immediately understood the significance of the living water to which He referred, but after walking a considerable distance with a large earthen pitcher of water on her head or shoulder, she at least appreciated its temporal indispensability if not its eternal symbolic significance (John 4:1–26).

Zechariah prophesied that when the Savior ushers in His Second Coming on the Mount of Olives, the mount will be cleft in twain, and "living waters shall go out from Jerusalem; half of them toward the former sea, and half of them toward the hinder sea" (Zechariah 14:8). Ezekiel also prophesied that these living waters would issue from the threshold of the temple and would flow eastward into the desert toward the Dead Sea. He prophesied that these waters would eventually become "a river that could not be passed over . . . which being brought forth into the sea, the waters shall be healed . . . and every thing shall live whither the river cometh" (Ezekiel 47:4, 8–9).

If the living water can heal the Dead Sea, the living water can certainly heal a withering marriage, a wilting testimony, a drooping relationship between neighbors or business associates, or alienation among siblings. The living water does, indeed, represent the love of God, and those who drink deeply from that water are able to sing the song of redeeming love.

Nephi continues the interpretation of his father's dream by a heavenly ministrant:

"And the angel said unto me again: Look and behold the condescension of God! And I looked and beheld the Redeemer of the world, of whom my father had spoken; and I also beheld the prophet who should prepare the way before him. And the Lamb of God went forth and was baptized of him; and after he was baptized, I beheld the heavens open, and the Holy Ghost come down out of heaven and abide upon him in the form of a dove. . . .

"And he spake unto me again, saying: Look! And I looked, and I beheld the Lamb of God going forth among the children of men. And I beheld multitudes of people who were sick, and who were afflicted with all manner of diseases, and with devils and unclean spirits; and the angel spake and showed all these things unto me. And they were healed by the power of the Lamb of God; and the devils and the unclean spirits were cast out.

"And it came to pass that the angel spake unto me again, saying: Look! And I looked and beheld the Lamb of God, that he was taken by the people; yea, the Son of the everlasting God was judged of the world; and I saw and bear record" (1 Nephi 11:26–27, 31–32).

"And the world, because of their iniquity, shall judge him to be a thing of naught; wherefore they scourge him, and he suffereth it; and they smite him, and he suffereth it. Yea, they spit upon him, and he suffereth it, because of his loving kindness and his long-suffering towards the children of men" (1 Nephi 19:9).

"And I, Nephi, saw that he was lifted up upon the cross and slain for the sins of the world" (1 Nephi 11:33).

A THING OF NAUGHT

I know a stalwart brother in the British Isles who deals in secondhand furniture and antiquated books. When an elderly person passes away, it is not uncommon for the next of kin to give him a call, requesting an estimate on the value of the furniture, books, and other items belonging to the deceased. The following scenario repeats itself weekly in many homes throughout England.

This brother arrives at the home with his truck and a couple of assistants. Family members direct them to load certain pieces of furniture into the truck and to leave other items behind. When it comes to books, the relatives often say, "Just pack them up and take them—they're all rather old." Time and again, he finds among those books the old family Bible, complete with several generations of genealogy in the front or middle pages. My friend will often ask the children of the deceased whether someone is interested in keeping this family treasure. In nearly every instance, none of the children or other relatives expresses any interest in keeping the Bible. Just as Nephi prophesied, they judge Him to be a thing of naught.

We should hold the prophets of the Book of Mormon in extraordinarily high esteem. Several centuries before the Savior's birth, they testified of Him with a certitude as if He had already come. Nephi declared, "We talk of Christ, we rejoice in Christ, we preach of Christ, we prophesy of Christ, and we write according to our prophecies, that our children may know to what source they may look for a remission of their sins" (2 Nephi 25:26). He further taught his posterity, speaking in the present tense of an event that would happen six centuries later, that the Savior "doeth not anything save it be for the benefit of the world; for he loveth the world, even that he layeth down his own life that he may draw all men unto him. Wherefore, he commandeth none that they shall not partake of his salvation" (2 Nephi 26:24).

Notwithstanding the surety of Nephi's testimony of the Savior's loving-kindness, Nephi, like most of us, seemed to pose the introspective questions: If I know what I know, why do I do as I do? Knowing what I know, why don't I do all the things I'm supposed to do?

One of the great sources of inspiration in the Book of Mormon is the disclosure of personal weakness by its prophets. We take no comfort knowing of their challenges, but as we learn how they overcame their struggles, their lives become a source of inspiration and encouragement to us all because "they which preach the gospel . . . live of the gospel" (1 Corinthians 9:14). Overcoming their weaknesses is what causes each of them to sing the song of redeeming love, for "it is by grace that we are saved, after all we can do" (2 Nephi 25:23). Their over-coming of *their* weaknesses gives each of us added strength, with a lot of help from above, to overcome *our* weaknesses.

Life in the desert was not easy. After following his father, Lehi, into the wilderness, Nephi and his brothers were asked to return to Jerusalem to procure from Laban the record contained on the brass plates. To help interest Laban in their record-extraction program, the brothers brought with them their family's valuable possessions. Upon seeing these possessions, Laban wished to keep the brass plates *and* their valuables, so he commanded his servants to slay Lehi's sons. As Nephi put it, "We were obliged to leave behind our property." They fled to the safety of a cave, having lost the first round (1 Nephi 3:26).

When players on a losing football team begin to realize that they may not have enough time to come from behind and win a ballgame, they sometimes take out their frustrations on their opponents. They begin blocking harder than they need to, tackling the running back out of bounds, roughing the kicker, violently sacking the quarterback, grabbing face masks, piling on after a tackle, or engaging in brutal pass interference.

Psychologists describe these behaviors in terms of "frustration-aggression" or "displaced aggression." Perhaps this explains in part why, after the brothers narrowly escaped with their lives, Laman and Lemuel became outraged with their father for sending them into harm's way. They also became

angry with Nephi for insisting that they remain loyal to their
father's instructions. Venting their frustrations, the two older
brothers began ruthlessly beating their younger brothers with
a rod. The beating was so severe that it was stopped by an
angel of the Lord, who may well have been dispatched to save
the lives of Nephi and Sam (1 Nephi 3:28–29).

Even with the passage of a considerable length of time,
Laman's animosity toward Nephi and Lehi was fomented to
such a degree that he proposed to Lemuel and the sons of
Ishmael that they slay the two prophets (1 Nephi 16:37.) The
intent of their hearts was known to both their brother and their
father, for Nephi later accused them of having sought to take
away their father's life (1 Nephi 17:44). Lehi, in turn, remon-
strated with his older sons for having sought to take away
Nephi's life, adding that "he hath suffered much sorrow because
of you" (2 Nephi 1:24).

After the Lord had commanded Nephi to construct a ship,
Nephi's brethren murmured and mocked him so much that
Nephi "was exceedingly sorrowful because of the hardness of
their hearts" (1 Nephi 17:18–19). Like the barnyard animals in
the *The Little Red Hen,* Laman and Lemuel were not too helpful, at first anyway, in building the ship. They were, nevertheless, willing to board the vessel after it had been completed. But
once they found themselves on uncharted waters and unsettled
seas, Nephi's brothers again treated him harshly, binding him
so tightly with cords that after four days his wrists and ankles
were severely swollen (1 Nephi 18:11–15). Eventually they
released him.

After their arrival in the promised land, and not long after
Lehi's death and burial, Nephi's brothers resumed their mur-
muring against him and openly announced their intentions
to slay him so they would "not be afflicted more because of
his words" (2 Nephi 5:3). These murderous threats were so

serious that the Lord warned Nephi to flee into the wilderness for his safety.

Nephi's writing is a great source of strength to any and all who have been placed in a particularly tough classroom here on earth and whose customized curriculum challenges them to the limit. Through it all, Nephi "did frankly forgive them all that they had done" (1 Nephi 7:21).

In the midst of all these afflictions, Nephi opens his heart to us as he writes "the things of [his] soul" (2 Nephi 4:15). What follows is unvarnished honesty, meekness, and candid self-assessment. He makes no excuses for his weaknesses but offers a humble plea for help from on high and issues a grateful acknowledgment for his many blessings. Nephi's psalm is a song of redeeming love:

"Behold, my soul delighteth in the things of the Lord; and my heart pondereth continually upon the things which I have seen and heard.

"Nevertheless, notwithstanding the great goodness of the Lord, in showing me his great and marvelous works, my heart exclaimeth: O wretched man that I am! Yea, my heart sorroweth because of my flesh; my soul grieveth because of my iniquities.

"I am encompassed about, because of the temptations and the sins which do so easily beset me. And when I desire to rejoice, my heart groaneth because of my sins; nevertheless, I know in whom I have trusted.

"My God hath been my support; he hath led me through mine afflictions in the wilderness; and he hath preserved me upon the waters of the great deep.

"He hath filled me with his love, even unto the consuming of my flesh. He hath confounded mine enemies, unto the causing of them to quake before me.

"Behold, he hath heard my cry by day, and he hath given

me knowledge by visions in the nighttime. And by day have I waxed bold in mighty prayer before him; yea, my voice have I sent up on high; and angels came down and ministered unto me.

"And upon the wings of his Spirit hath my body been carried away upon exceedingly high mountains. And mine eyes have beheld great things, yea, even too great for man; therefore I was bidden that I should not write them.

"O then, if I have seen so great things, if the Lord in his condescension unto the children of men hath visited men in so much mercy, why should my heart weep and my soul linger in the valley of sorrow, and my flesh waste away, and my strength slacken, because of mine afflictions?

"And why should I yield to sin, because of my flesh? Yea, why should I give way to temptations, that the evil one have place in my heart to destroy my peace and afflict my soul? Why am I angry because of mine enemy?

"Awake, my soul! No longer droop in sin. Rejoice, O my heart, and give place no more for the enemy of my soul. Do not anger again because of mine enemies. Do not slacken my strength because of mine afflictions.

"Rejoice, O my heart, and cry unto the Lord, and say: O Lord, I will praise thee forever; yea, my soul will rejoice in thee, my God, and the rock of my salvation.

"O Lord, wilt thou redeem my soul? Wilt thou deliver me out of the hands of mine enemies? Wilt thou make me that I may shake at the appearance of sin?

"May the gates of hell be shut continually before me, because that my heart is broken and my spirit is contrite! O Lord, wilt thou not shut the gates of thy righteousness before me. . . . O Lord, wilt thou encircle me around in the robe of thy righteousness! . . . O Lord, I have trusted in thee, and I will trust in thee forever. . . .

"Yea, I know that God will give liberally to him that asketh. Yea, my God will give me, if I ask not amiss; therefore I will lift up my voice unto thee; yea, I will cry unto thee, my God, the rock of my righteousness. Behold, my voice shall forever ascend up unto thee, my rock and mine everlasting God. Amen" (2 Nephi 4:16–35).

Nephi's candid disclosure of his sporadic self-doubts and susceptibility to sin is perfectly understandable in the context of his life's experiences. Many, if not all, of his greatest trials originated within his family circle. His older brothers were not only spiritually rebellious but also very emotionally and physically abusive to Nephi. As Lehi became older and physically weaker, the lot fell to Nephi to provide leadership for the entire extended family. His efforts were met with resistance on nearly every side. Thus, when he confessed to being beset by temptation, he disclosed feelings that any other mortal would have experienced in similar circumstances. Still, he knew that he must overcome those feelings and temptations, and he realized that with the Lord's help, overcoming is not only possible but expected.

At the close of Nephi's ministry, he admonished his beloved brethren, those with listening ears, to "follow the Son, with full purpose of heart, acting no hypocrisy and no deception before God, but with real intent, repenting of your sins, witnessing unto the Father that ye are willing to take upon you the name of Christ, by baptism" (2 Nephi 31:13).

"Wherefore, do the things which I have told you I have seen that your Lord and your Redeemer should do; for, for this cause have they been shown unto me, that ye might know the gate by which ye should enter. For the gate by which ye should enter is repentance and baptism by water; and then cometh a remission of your sins by fire and by the Holy Ghost" (2 Nephi 31:17).

"I glory in plainness; I glory in truth; I glory in my Jesus, for he hath redeemed my soul from hell" (2 Nephi 33:6).

"WHY DIDN'T YOU FIND ME?"

Karl Trinkl is a native Hungarian who left his homeland at age seventeen, immigrating first to Germany and then, thirty years ago, to Austria. Despite recently celebrating his seventy-eighth birthday, he still has a full head of coal black hair and a zest for life more common among the young. He is a small man whose heart is larger than life and whose love for others knows no bounds. This natural inclination to serve others led him into contact with the missionaries in 1977.

As he stood, slightly inebriated, at a pedestrian lane on a busy street in Vienna, he noticed a young mother struggling to cross the street with her shopping packages and a stroller containing her young child. Immediately he rushed to her aid and assisted her across the street. In gratitude for his kindness, this young mother jotted down the address of the Church in Vienna and invited Karl to attend meetings the following Sunday. In a week or two, he accepted the invitation and came to Church, where he met the full-time missionaries, who found him to be receptive to their message. At the time of his conversion, he was working as a cook in a restaurant and had no apartment of his own. His generous employer allowed him to sleep in the kitchen "between the pots and pans and all the dishes."

Before Karl's baptism, his entire life had lacked a sense of direction and purpose. Unlike Nephi, he was not afflicted by older brothers who beat him up or threatened to murder him; however, the vicissitudes of life had continually beaten up on him. He had floated aimlessly from one job to another, working mostly in restaurants. Alcohol had become a temporary anesthetic against the pains of life. But six months after his baptism, Brother Trinkl had his own apartment, and life began to take a dramatic turn for the better. He was assigned to home teach a single sister named Margarethe, and not long after his first home teaching visit to her, they were married. Throughout the years, the two of them have enjoyed serving as stake missionaries in Vienna and as temple workers in the Swiss Temple.

Our family met Brother and Sister Trinkl in 1984 as we served in the presidency of the Austria Vienna Mission. In the autumn of that year, the executives of National Hungarian Television decided to produce a television program about an exotic group of people living in western America called "Mormons." They sent a film crew to interview dozens of people and to film Church meetings, family home evenings, and a wide variety of other Church and family activities. After a month in Utah, the TV crew members returned to Budapest, where their thousands of feet of film were edited into a four-part miniseries called "The Mormons of Utah," which was broadcast in late 1985.[1]

Following the broadcast, our mission office in Vienna began receiving dozens of requests for information that had been forwarded to us from Church headquarters. At that time we had no missionaries assigned to Hungary, and so we were faced with a delightful dilemma: How could we teach all these interested people when we had no Hungarian-speaking missionaries? As the mission president, I turned to Brother Trinkl. I called him to be my missionary companion in visiting several Hungarians who wanted to know more about the Church. Many of these people spoke either German or English, and I was able to assume most of the responsibility for teaching them. But for those who spoke only Hungarian, reliable Brother Trinkl became their teacher.

Eventually we were able to locate a young Hungarian-speaking missionary from Canada, Elder Zolton Nagy-Kovac, serving in Germany, and a linguistically gifted missionary from

Lausanne, Switzerland, Elder Jean Marc Frey, serving in Austria. They were transferred to Hungary to assist Elder Wayne and Sister Linnea Johnson, a senior missionary couple who had arrived to provide leadership training in Hungary.

One day as Brother Trinkl and I were driving through the Hungarian plains on one of our trips to Budapest, he asked me where I had served my mission as a young man. I told him I had served in the South German Mission and had spent much of my time in the city of Stuttgart. This news left him animated. "And when did you labor in Stuttgart?" he asked with intense interest. "From autumn of 1960 to spring of 1963," I replied matter-of-factly. I was not prepared for his reaction to this tidbit of seemingly trivial information. With unrestrained vigor he exclaimed, "That's when I lived in Stuttgart!"

Then, to my great astonishment he suddenly clutched my arm and cried almost in agony, "Bruder Condie, why didn't you find me in 1963?" His outburst caused me to chuckle, and I replied, "Bruder Trinkl, Stuttgart had 600,000 people in 1963. How could I possibly have found you?" After a rather long pause, he broke the silence. He was not accusing or castigating me, but he said in his own soft way, "If you had found me in 1963, I would not have had to wait fourteen more years to join the Church in 1977 in Vienna."

I have often been haunted by Brother Trinkl's indictment, and I fear that when I pass beyond the veil I may be accosted by many others who will ask, "Why didn't you find me?"

Brother Trinkl's life went from meaningless to meaningful in a matter of days following his introduction to the gospel. Before his baptism, he saw life's vicissitudes as vicious intrusions engendering feelings of hopelessness. But now, being armed with faith in Jesus Christ, cleansed from past sins, and ordained to priesthood power, Karl Trinkl realizes that life's disappointments and pain are part of an opposition in *all* things.

They are part of what Elder Neal A. Maxwell calls the Lord's customized curriculum that leads us back into God's presence.[2]

On one of our trips to Debrecen, Hungary, Brother Trinkl and I visited a family who had become interested in the Church after their son was baptized while living in Vienna. The family had invited two friends into their home to participate in our gospel discussion. As was often the case in Hungary, the discussion was preceded by a meal of soup, salad, sausage, and potatoes, followed by dessert and a few drinks of juice and mineral water.

After the meal, I began the discussion, speaking in German. Brother Trinkl translated my first sentence briefly. My second statement took him a bit longer to translate. I was pleased that he felt comfortable enough to add his own commentary. But by the time we reached the third principle of the first discussion, he had forgotten me altogether and had begun explaining the gospel in his own unsystematic way. At times he was serious and at times he laughed, but he always he spoke with great enthusiasm. The Hungarians affectionately called Brother Trinkl "Karçsibacsi," or Little Uncle Karl.

These people knew nothing of the Church, but they listened to Uncle Karl intently. As they saw the love he had for them and for the gospel, his enthusiasm became contagious. Like water lilies unfolding in the warmth of the morning sun, they began to relax and enjoy the Spirit they felt so strongly.

We had planned to close our discussion with prayer and then leave while they felt the Spirit. So after our prayer, I suggested that we leave, but Uncle Karl countered with a proposal that we sing a few Hungarian folk songs before departing. And so we sang plaintive, melancholy melodies that expressed the struggle with the land and the war within oneself.

The hour grew late, but Uncle Karl volunteered to sing one last song, "Granada," in his operatic tenor voice. Our hosts

were overjoyed by his spontaneous outburst and were somewhat surprised by his talent. As we made our way to the door,
they kissed us on each cheek and invited us to visit them again
on our next visit to Hungary.

As we drove home, I reflected upon what had happened.
What could these gracious hosts have learned and remembered
about the gospel after our discussion? The answer came
quietly. Perhaps, I thought, Brother Trinkl's enthusiastic teaching, love, animated singing, and good humor taught the lesson
that lies at the heart of all our gospel teaching: Man is that he
might have joy.

The zest for life in confronting difficult circumstances char-
acterizes Hungarians. Brother Trinkl is not unique among his
countrymen. Most lack only the one thing: the restored gospel
of Jesus Christ.[3]

Karl Trinkl has learned the veracity of the Lord's promise
that when we lose ourselves in the service of others, we find
ourselves. In other words, we find meaning and purpose and
joy in our lives.

NOTES

1. Dorothy Stowe, "Film Makers Satisy Europe's Curiosity," *Church
News,* 11 November 1984, 10.

2. Maxwell, "Thanks Be to God," *Ensign,* July 1982, 52.

3. Spencer J. Condie, "Teaching the Gospel with Karçibaci," *Ensign,*
June 1990, 14.

THREE

Jacob's Song of Reconciliation

Wherefore, my beloved brethren, reconcile yourselves to the will of God, and not to the will of the devil and the flesh; and remember, after ye are reconciled unto God, that it is only in and through the grace of God that ye are saved. Wherefore, may God raise you from death by the power of the resurrection, and also from everlasting death by the power of the atonement, that ye may be received into the eternal kingdom of God, that ye may praise him through grace divine. Amen (2 Nephi 10:24–25).

Though father Lehi found that his two oldest sons were not teachable, he could have taken great comfort in the fact that his son Jacob was a prize pupil in listening, applying, and perpetuating his father's teachings. Jacob, because of his tender age, had perhaps been somewhat insulated from much of the affliction heaped upon Lehi and Nephi by Laman and Lemuel, his older brothers. In his writing, Jacob did not dwell on tribulation; rather, he focused on the importance of serving the Lord and becoming unspotted from the sins of the world. He also reflected a deep understanding of the Atonement as it was taught by Nephi and his father. Just as his father taught him, he taught others the song of redeeming love:

"O how great the goodness of our God, who prepareth a way for our escape from the grasp of this awful monster; yea, that monster, death and hell, which I call the death of the body, and also the death of the spirit" (2 Nephi 9:10).

"O then, my beloved brethren, come unto the Lord, the Holy One. Remember that his paths are righteous. Behold, the way for man is narrow, but it lieth in a straight course before him, and the keeper of the gate is the Holy One of Israel; and he employeth no servant there; and there is none other way save it be by the gate; for he cannot be deceived, for the Lord God is his name" (2 Nephi 9:41).

"Wherefore, my beloved brethren, reconcile yourselves to the will of God, and not to the will of the devil and the flesh; and remember, after ye are reconciled unto God, that it is only in and through the grace of God that ye are saved.

"Wherefore, may God raise you from death by the power of the resurrection, and also from everlasting death by the power of the atonement, that ye may be received into the eternal kingdom of God, that ye may praise him through grace divine. Amen" (2 Nephi 10:24–25).

"Wherefore, beloved brethren, be reconciled unto him through the atonement of Christ, his Only Begotten Son, and ye may obtain a resurrection, according to the power of the resurrection which is in Christ, and be presented as the first-fruits of Christ unto God, having faith, and obtained a good hope of glory in him before he manifesteth himself in the flesh" (Jacob 4:11).

The process of reconciliation lies at the heart of the gathering of scattered Israel. Both Jacob and Nephi were familiar with Isaiah's words regarding the time of reconciliation that would come when scattered Israel would return to the God of

Abraham, Isaac, and Jacob. At that time, the Lord revealed, "shall the Jews look upon me and say: What are these wounds in thine hands and in thy feet? Then shall they know that I am the Lord; for I will say unto them: These wounds are the wounds with which I was wounded in the house of my friends. I am he who was lifted up. I am Jesus that was crucified. I am the Son of God. . . . And then shall the heathen nations be redeemed" (D&C 45:51, 52, 54).

"WHY DID I WAIT SO LONG?"

For more than two decades, we lived in a modest home in a quiet neighborhood in Provo. Two of our good neighbors down the street were Lois and Richard Levin. Lois had been a member of the Church her entire life and reared her children as Latter-day Saints. Richard had been reared in a Roman Catholic home, and he was bound and determined never to leave the Catholic faith. Though he had a friendly disposition toward his LDS friends, he made it abundantly clear that he was not interested in changing his religious affiliation.

A few years ago, my wife, Dorothea, and I felt impressed to begin visiting Lois and Richard. We used to take walks around the neighborhood on cool summer evenings, and on one of these occasions we found ourselves on the Levins' front porch. Lois and Richard invited us inside for a visit. After discussing the weather, sports, and politics, Richard indicated that we were welcome to return but that religion was off-limits as a point of discussion. I said, "Well, Richard, that kind of puts me at a disadvantage, because that's all I ever talk about." On the way home, Dorothea said, "Honey, you've got to learn to be more gentle with people and not be so abrupt and direct with them."

A few weeks later it was apple-picking time. We filled a large plastic bucket with red delicious apples from our tree and headed for the Levins. We continued our visits over the next several months, with but few references to religion. After Richard and Lois took a Caribbean cruise, they invited us over to see photographs of their vacation. It was not long before Christmastime rolled around. When we returned to the Levins with some Christmas goodies Dorothea had baked, Richard was warming but not quite ready.

After the New Year began, we asked Richard directly if he was ready to receive the missionary discussions. He indicated that he had had a few discussions several years before but that the experience had been unsatisfactory. We let the matter drop, but we kept up our visits through February, March, and April. Richard's heart softened after he attended a missionary homecoming for a granddaughter who had served in Argentina. One Friday evening in May he called us out of the blue.

"Is that offer for the missionary discussions still good?" he asked softly. "Of course, dear brother," I replied after picking myself up off the floor.

At the appointed day and hour, we explained to Richard that when we discuss sacred things we need the Spirit of the Lord to be with us. I said, "You're the patriarch of this home, Richard. Who would you like to pray?" He asked me to offer the prayer. The Spirit was strong, and the discussion went well, including his acceptance of Joseph Smith's vision of the Father and the Son. The next week we returned for the second discussion. "Who should pray tonight?" I asked. "Dorothea, please," he responded. Again, the Lord's Spirit was evident as we experienced what President Gordon B. Hinckley observed: "The Holy Ghost is the Testifier of Truth, who can teach men things they cannot teach one another."[1]

When we returned for the third discussion, we again asked Richard who should begin our discussion with prayer. He responded, "I guess it's my turn." The Spirit had been stirring within his heart, and his prayer in the presence of others reflected that he had privately, prayerfully been pleading with the Lord for answers to his questions and concerns. Needless to say, our ensuing discussion on the restoration of priesthood keys went well.

During the fourth discussion, we encountered some bumps in the road. Actually, we hit some giant potholes. Investigators are frequently receptive throughout the first three discussions, but during the fourth lesson the missionaries ask them to begin making significant changes in their lives. Many latter-day investigators are like the interested individuals in Christ's day who followed the Savior in order to observe firsthand some of His miracles. They were willing to listen to Him teach them on the hillside, and they were grateful to be fed miraculously and amply from five barley loaves and two fishes. But when the Savior began challenging them to change their lives, "many of his disciples went back, and walked no more with him" (John 6:66).

The fourth discussion includes the plan of eternal progression, the gift of moral agency, and the recognition that our bodies are temples of God and should be kept clean. We discuss the law of chastity and the Word of Wisdom, and then we challenge investigators to abide by commandments related to these laws.

Several years before we met Richard, he had been a heavy smoker. His physician, however, had warned him that he must relinquish his habit or die of emphysema. He immediately gave up cigarettes. Coffee, on the other hand, was another matter. "I don't drink coffee all day long," Richard explained. "I just need two cups in the morning to get my old engine started. Surely you wouldn't keep me out of the Church for only two cups of coffee."

"Richard," I responded, "I'm in sales, not management. I

just preach the gospel; I don't make the commandments." Once again, on the way home, Dorothea chided me for being more direct than diplomatic, and I had a worrisome night's sleep, fearing that perhaps Richard was going to elude the gospel net.

When I returned home from the office the next evening, I was expecting a kiss from my wife. Instead, she brushed me aside and said, "Richard needs to see you right away." My heart sank. I feared he was cooling down and had perhaps decided to call off the rest of the discussions. I hurriedly walked down the street and knocked on the Levins' door. Richard had a wry smile on his face as he opened the door.

"Did Dorothea tell you what happened this afternoon?" he asked. "No," I responded, "she didn't even give me a kiss when I came home. She said I needed to see you right away, so here I am."

"Well," Richard began, slowly searching for the right beginning, "last night you were so hard on me about drinking coffee that I decided I'd drop by and see Dorothea this afternoon to see if she'd let me join the Church with two cups of coffee."

"So, what did she tell you?" I asked.

"She said, 'Richard, I promise you that if you will faithfully live the Word of Wisdom, you will have better health and more strength and energy than you have had in years.' And as she was talking to me, I started to cry. Can you imagine that, a grown man crying in front of a woman?"

I responded quietly, "That was the Spirit, Richard, testifying that the things she was teaching you were true."

"I know," he said softly.

After a brief time of reflection, I broke the silence. "So where do we go from here?"

"I guess we need the next discussion," he replied enthusiastically.

"We'll be talking about tithing," I said with a smile.

"That's okay," he said. "I know all about tithing. It's just those two cups of coffee that bother me."

We held the fifth discussion about becoming like Christ through living the law of the fast, lifting others through generous fast offerings, faithfully paying tithing, and keeping all the other commandments. The sixth discussion was uneventful as we discussed the blessings and obligations of membership in the kingdom of God. The zone leaders then interviewed Richard for baptism.

The baptismal service was one of the finest we have ever attended. The speakers' remarks were inspirational and heartfelt. Lois and her children had primed the grandchildren to sing "I Am a Child of God,"[2] which melted our hearts. The bishop asked Richard if he would like to bear his testimony, but his head was a fountain of tears and he respectfully declined.

A week or two later, Richard was ordained a priest in the Aaronic Priesthood. Several weeks afterward, as Dorothea and I entered the chapel, the bishop informed us that Richard had been invited to administer the sacrament. "Inasmuch as this is his first time, he's very nervous," the bishop said. "So I would appreciate it if you would assist him today." It was a great honor to be seated at the sacrament table with this newly baptized brother whom I had grown to love so well.

This was a fast and testimony Sunday, and following the administration of the sacrament we gained a glimpse of heaven as various members of the ward rose to their feet and expressed their love and support for Richard Levin. Some asked his forgiveness for not having been better examples. Others expressed their regrets that they had not tried harder and earlier to interest him in the gospel. But most reaffirmed the love ward members had for each other, and they offered a warm welcome to Richard, who had long been our neighbor but now belonged to a community of the Saints.

The bishop gave Richard a special calling, supervising home teaching in the ward. His duty was to phone all the home teachers several times a month to remind them to visit their families. My eighty-five-year-old father, who lived across the street from us, told me one day, "Son, that was a mistake to baptize Richard Levin." I knew my dad was, in fact, fond of Richard, so I took his remark with several grains of salt. "Why, is that?" I asked. "Well," my dad said, "I always get my home teaching done each and every month without a phone call, but now he calls me two or three times a month to see if I've got it done yet!"

Richard had recently retired and had plenty of time for reading. After completing the Book of Mormon, he began reading the Doctrine and Covenants with great relish. As Dorothea and I continued our weekly visits, we were continually impressed by the depth of his questions and the profundity of his insights into the gospel. He was not just an avid reader; he was also a student and a thinker. His enthusiastic response to his church calling demonstrated that he was a doer as well.

Dorothea and I were given a new assignment in England, so our weekly contact was interrupted. But when we returned home for general conference, we went with Richard and Lois to the Provo Temple, where they received their temple endowments and I had the privilege of sealing them for time and all eternity. Richard had been well prepared to participate in the sacred ordinances, and the Spirit in the temple made for a wonderful experience. But as we left the temple grounds, Richard kept muttering in subdued tones, "Why did I wait so long? Why did I wait so long?"

Richard did more than magnify his home teaching calling. He caught the spirit of family history research, and he developed a great love for the temple, assuring that vicarious temple work was completed for numerous ancestors. When he recently passed away, he left behind a great legacy to his forty-five grandchildren and twenty great-grandchildren. He had not just been baptized into the Church; he had become a convert who underwent a mighty change of heart and learned well how to sing the song of redeeming love.

Richard left this mortal sphere aware of his indebtedness to the Savior and with the assurance that because he had truly repented of his sins, he was reconciled with God.

NOTES

1. Hinckley, "The Father, Son, and Holy Ghost," *Ensign*, March 1998, 7.

2. *Hymns*, no. 301.

FOUR

Enos' Song of Eternal Rest

And I soon go to the place of my rest, which is with my Redeemer; for I know that in him I shall rest. And I rejoice in the day when my mortal shall put on immortality, and shall stand before him; then shall I see his face with pleasure, and he will say unto me: Come unto me, ye blessed, there is a place prepared for you in the mansions of my Father. Amen (Enos 1:27).

Those with unforgiving hearts, unresolved sins, and unrequited egos are seldom, if ever, at rest. Righteous people, on the other hand, enjoy the reward of entering into the rest of the Lord. Enos, the son of Jacob, was such a person. He summoned the strength and courage to cast his burdens upon the Lord and then mustered the humility to report his experience in order to bless our lives:

"Behold, I went to hunt beasts in the forests; and the words which I had often heard my father speak concerning eternal life, and the joy of the saints, sunk deep into my heart.

"And my soul hungered; and I kneeled down before my Maker, and I cried unto him in mighty prayer and supplication for mine own soul; and all the day long did I cry unto him; yea, and when the night came I did still raise my voice high that it reached the heavens.

"And there came a voice unto me, saying: Enos, thy sins are forgiven thee, and thou shalt be blessed. And I, Enos, knew that God could not lie; wherefore, my guilt was swept away. And I said: Lord, how is it done?" (Enos 1:3–7).

As Enos received confirmation that his sins had been forgiven, his self-interest gave way to a concern for his brethren, the Nephites. As his cleansing became more complete, he even prayed "with many long strugglings" for his brethren, the Lamanites (Enos 1:11). Unless and until we have been forgiven, and we know we have been forgiven, we tend to think primarily of our own personal welfare. Such is the egocentricity of sin. But when we have been hollowed of our sins, we suddenly find room to be concerned for the welfare of others. That was Enos' experience. Though his contribution to the Book of Mormon is brief, it is profound, concluding with divine assurance:

"And I soon go to the place of my rest, which is with my Redeemer; for I know that in him I shall rest. And I rejoice in the day when my mortal shall put on immortality, and shall stand before him; then shall I see his face with pleasure, and he will say unto me: Come unto me, ye blessed, there is a place prepared for you in the mansions of my Father. Amen" (Enos 1:27).

HANDEL FINDS REST

George Frederick Handel was born in 1685 in the eastern German city of Halle an der Salle. He matured into a large man of boundless energy, a healthy appetite, and an adventuresome spirit. Handel spent some of his early years roaming restlessly about the northern German cities of Hannover, Lubeck, Berlin, and Hamburg, where he composed his first opera. Inasmuch as Italy was the operatic center of the world, he moved there and began to make a name for himself. His Italian opera, *Rodrigo,* was widely acclaimed, but on the crest of victory he decided to go to England to ply his wares.

British tastes for music were different from those in Italy or Germany. The British were reluctant to accept the operatic form of music sung in German or Italian, with plots often involving adultery and other forms of mischief. For several years, Handel's attempts at composing in England met with mixed success. In 1737, the prodigious composer finished his fourth opera within a period of twelve months, pushing himself to the very limit of his physical abilities. Handel was a corpulent man who paid more attention to work and food than to exercise. Not long after his fifty-second birthday, his secretary, Christopher Smith, discovered the composer lying on the floor, disoriented and gasping for breath.

Smith hurried down the street to fetch a Dr. Jenkins. After checking his patient's reflexes and getting no response from the seemingly lifeless right side of Handel's body, Dr. Jenkins pronounced the diagnosis: Handel had suffered a stroke. When Smith asked the doctor for his prognosis, Jenkins replied, "We may save the man—but the musician is lost forever. It seems to me that his brain has been permanently injured."[1]

For the next four months, Handel was completely immobile and incapable of speaking. In desperation, Dr. Jenkins proposed that his patient be transported to the thermal springs at Aix-la-Chapelle, Germany (Aachen), hoping that hot baths could bring about a dramatic change in Handel's condition. The caretakers at Aix-la-Chapelle warned Handel against staying in the hot water longer than three hours at a time, afraid that his doing so would strain his heart. But Handel wanted to compose again, and he insisted on remaining in the water

much longer—some times as long as nine hours. It was difficult to dissuade him once he had made up his Germanic mind.
Just one week after his arrival at the health spa, he was able to
take a few steps. A few days later, he could raise his right arm.

Eventually, as Handel was preparing to leave the city in
which he had miraculously regained his strength, he entered a
cathedral. With some trepidation, he began fingering the key-
board of the organ. Gradually, he became more and more confident in playing with both hands as glorious strains of music
filled both the cathedral and his soul. "I have come back from
Hades," he jubilantly proclaimed.[2]

He returned to London to the labor he loved as much as
life, composing six operas within a relatively short period of
time. As his strength and vigor returned, so did his creditors.
But his operatic efforts again met with less than a warm reception by the British public, which preferred the satirical and
comedic musical *Beggar's Opera* to Handel's ponderous *Saul* or
Israel in Egypt. Critics of his operatic works incited his creditors, who began dunning him on every side. In introspective
moments, Handel was beginning to wonder in the depths of
despondency, "Why did God permit my resurrection, only to
allow my fellow-men to bury me again?"[3]

At this juncture, the duke of Devonshire invited Handel to
compose a work that could be performed as a series of benefit
concerts for charities in Dublin. But because of pressure from
his creditors and rejection by his critics and the general public, "the mills of fantasy had ceased working. . . . There was
nothing to begin or to finish. Handel was faced with emptiness."[4]

After taking a long and tiring walk, Handel returned to his
apartment, where he found that someone had left him a white
parcel. Upon opening it, he discovered a manuscript from
a poet and previous collaborator, Charles Jennens, who had

provided the libretto for *Saul* and *Israel in Egypt*. The manuscript included numerous verses from scriptures foretelling the birth of Jesus Christ. It was to be an oratorio. In light of his previous failures and rejection, Handel was apprehensive at first as he began reading through the text, but the first words leapt from the page: "Comfort ye." The words seemed to dissipate the dark clouds that had been pressing upon him for so long. His emotions changed from depression to interest to excitement as he read of comfort, angelic proclamations, and a loving shepherd feeding his sheep. Then came the exultation: "Hallelujah."

Suddenly, inspiration began to flow, and melodies distilled upon Handel faster than he could write the notes on paper. He began composing on August 22, 1741, and for the next three weeks, he slept and ate little. On September 14, he concluded his single-minded task. The *Messiah* was completed, at least in preliminary form. At the conclusion of his work, Handel humbly acknowledged, "God has visited me."[5]

Not long after Handel temporarily moved to Dublin, two Irish gentlemen approached him regarding the possibility of making the first night's performance of the *Messiah* a benefit concert for charity. Handel indicated that profits from the first performance and all future performances "be donated to prisoners, orphans, and the sick. I have myself been a very sick man, and am now cured. I was a prisoner, and have been set free."[6]

Handel had been relieved of his restless quest for fame, fortune, and public praise, writing his crowning work for an earthly as well as a heavenly audience. The hollowing of a career as an operatic composer had led to the hallowing of his oratorio. The things that mattered most were no longer at the mercy of the things that mattered least. Handel, the restless composer, spent his remaining days at rest.

NOTES

1. Zweig, *The Tide of Fortune,* 104.
2. Zweig, 107.
3. Zweig, 108.
4. Zweig, 110.
5. Zweig, 121.
6. Zweig, 122.

FIVE

King Benjamin's Song of Remission of Sins

---

*Always retain in remembrance, the greatness of God,
and your own nothingness, and his goodness and long-
suffering towards you, . . . If ye do this ye shall always
rejoice, and be filled with the love of God, and always retain
a remission of your sins; and ye shall grow in the knowledge
of the glory of him that created you, or in the knowledge of
that which is just and true (Mosiah 4:11–12).*

More than two thousand years ago, a large congregation of
Saints gathered around the temple in the land of
Zarahemla to hear one of the greatest sermons ever recorded in
holy writ. Four times King Benjamin reminded his listeners
that he spoke the words given to him by an angel of God
(Mosiah 3:2; 4:1; 4:11; 5:5).

"For behold, the time cometh, and is not far distant, that
with power, the Lord Omnipotent who reigneth, who was, and
is from all eternity to all eternity, shall come down from heaven
among the children of men, and shall dwell in a tabernacle of
clay, and shall go forth amongst men, working mighty miracles,
such as healing the sick, raising the dead, causing the lame to

walk, the blind to receive their sight, and the deaf to hear, and curing all manner of diseases.

"And he shall cast out devils, or the evil spirits which dwell in the hearts of the children of men. And lo, he shall suffer temptations, and pain of body, hunger, thirst, and fatigue, even more than man can suffer, except it be unto death; for behold, blood cometh from every pore, so great shall be his anguish for the wickedness and the abominations of his people.

"And he shall be called Jesus Christ, the Son of God, the Father of heaven and earth, the Creator of all things from the beginning; and his mother shall be called Mary.

"And lo, he cometh unto his own, that salvation might come unto the children of men even through faith on his name; and even after all this they shall consider him a man, and say that he hath a devil, and shall scourge him, and shall crucify him.

"And he shall rise the third day from the dead; and behold, he standeth to judge the world; and behold, all these things are done that a righteous judgment might come upon the children of men.

"For behold he judgeth, and his judgment is just; and the infant perisheth not that dieth in his infancy; but men drink damnation to their own souls except they humble themselves and become as little children, and believe that salvation was, and is, and is to come, in and through the atoning blood of Christ, the Lord Omnipotent" (Mosiah 3:5–10, 18).

After listening to King Benjamin's stirring sermon, the vast congregation cried in unison, "O have mercy, and apply the atoning blood of Christ that we may receive forgiveness of our sins." In response to their pleas, "the Spirit of the Lord came upon them, and they were filled with joy" (Mosiah 4:2–3). One of the hallmarks of being forgiven of our sins is a feeling of joy, for Alma declared that "wickedness never was happiness" (Alma 41:10).

As they recognized the goodness of God, the people of Zarahemla also experienced a "peace of conscience" and were "filled with the love of God," two further manifestations that they had been forgiven (Mosiah 4:3, 12). An additional indicator of their remission of sins is that they did not "have a mind to injure one another" (Mosiah 4:13), nor did they permit their children to "transgress the laws of God, and fight and quarrel one with another" (Mosiah 4:14). Yet another token, King Benjamin told the people, is a desire to help those in need, a willingness to "impart of the substance that ye have one to another" (Mosiah 4:14, 21).

At the conclusion of his inspired address, the people believed all his words, experienced a mighty change of heart, and had "no more disposition to do evil, but to do good continually" (Mosiah 5:2). Perhaps of all the evidence of true conversion and remission of sins, the disposition to no longer do evil but to do good continually is the most significant.

THE TEN COMMANDMENTS AND THE SERMON ON THE MOUNT

Disposition constitutes a significant distinction between the Ten Commandments and the Savior's Sermon on the Mount. The Ten Commandments prohibit certain behaviors, such as murder, adultery, and profanity, but the Sermon on the Mount forbids even the dispositions leading to these evil behaviors, such as anger, lust, and any swearing at all (Matthew 5:21–37; 3 Nephi 12:21–37). The Beatitudes encourage the development of dispositions toward meekness, mercy, purity of heart, and many other godly attributes (Matthew 5:3–12; 3 Nephi 12:3–12). When we have a disposition to do good continually, we will naturally "abstain from all appearance of evil"

(1 Thessalonians 5:22) and not "look upon sin save it [be] with abhorrence" (Alma 13:12).

King Benjamin cautioned his people: "I cannot tell you all the things whereby ye may commit sin. . . . But this much I can tell you, that if ye do not watch yourselves, and your *thoughts,* and your *words,* and your *deeds*, and observe the commandments of God, and continue in the faith of what ye have heard concerning the coming of our Lord, even unto the end of your lives, ye must perish." He then lovingly admonished the Saints to "remember, and perish not" (Mosiah 4:29–30; emphasis added).

CULTIVATING DISPOSITIONS

Many of our personal dispositions mirror the cultural traditions that we internalize during our maturation. The widespread consumption of alcohol, immodesty of dress and behavior, and cohabitation without marriage are but a few examples of cultural traditions alien to the spirit of the gospel. So it is that the "wicked one cometh and taketh away light and truth, through disobedience, from the children of men, and because of the tradition of their fathers" (D&C 93:39).

Incorrect traditions seem natural because many people in a given society engage in such behaviors, but the commandments of God are based upon revealed truth, not popular preference. Thus, King Benjamin warned his people that "the natural man is an enemy to God." He exhorted them to put off the natural man or, in other words, to reject unholy traditions and to undergo a "mighty change" in their natural dispositions by yielding "to the enticings of the Holy Spirit" (Mosiah 3:19).

Sometimes Latter-day Saints become so fond of certain traditions within the Church that change in a given policy or procedure becomes a test of their faith. They believe in continuous revelation as long as it does not involve change.

The seeds of our disposition toward obedience and faith are largely sown by our desires. In teaching the wayward Zoramites how they could gain a knowledge of the truth, Alma admonished them to "exercise a particle of faith," and if they could "no more than desire to believe, [to] let this desire work in [them]" (Alma 32:27). What begins as a fleeting desire, when cultivated and pursued long enough, becomes a habitual form of thought or behavior.

President Joseph Fielding Smith observed, "It is just as easy to form good habits as it is to form evil ones."[1] Elder James E. Talmage also contended that "a thoroughly truthful man cannot culpably lie; nevertheless, his insurance against falsehood is not that of external compulsion, but of internal restraint due to his cultivated companionship of the spirit of truth."[2]

Alma poignantly explained the eternal consequences of desires and dispositions to his wayward son, Corianton. "In the last day it shall be restored unto him according to his deeds," Alma taught of whosoever rejects the gospel's call to give up our natural dispositions. "If he has desired to do evil, and has not repented in his days, behold, evil shall be done unto him, according to the restoration of God" (Alma 42:27–28). The person who fails to pay an honest tithe has a disposition similar to the individual who robs a bank—the main differences are the victims and the methods. The Lord asks, "Will a man rob God? Yet ye have robbed me. But ye say, Wherein have we robbed thee? In tithes and offerings" (Malachi 3:8).

Individuals who have difficulty controlling their anger toward a neighbor have a disposition similar to that of a dictator who would wage war against a neighboring nation. Internet and television addicts who surf Satan's smutty smorgasbord of pornography have the same inclinations as those who actually commit immoral acts; their dispositions differ only by degree.

James described this process in sequential detail: "Every

man is tempted, when he is drawn away of his own lust, and enticed. Then when lust hath conceived, it bringeth forth sin: and sin, when it is finished, bringeth forth death" (James 1:14–15). Our dispositions are generally manifest in our behaviors, and thus James gives each of us the challenge: "Shew me thy faith without thy works, and I will shew thee my faith by my works" (James 2:18).

Some potential missionaries or couples planning to be sealed in the temple are occasionally distraught to learn that recent transgressions will require them to wait a year or longer before claiming the blessings of a mission or temple marriage. They wonder if their fasting, tears, and prayers are of no avail in demonstrating a broken heart and a contrite spirit as they ask, "Why must we wait so long?"

This seems a fair question, especially in light of the Lord's assurance: "By this ye may know if a man repenteth of his sins—behold, he will confess them and forsake them" (D&C 58:43). Confession is a crucial prerequisite to forgiveness, but a disposition to no more do evil must follow confession. This cultivation is evidenced by completely forsaking sin, and this requires the passage of time. Peter graphically likened those who briefly repent but do not overcome a disposition toward evil to "the dog [that] is turned to his own vomit again; and the sow that was washed to her wallowing in the mire" (2 Peter 2:22). In latter-day revelation, the Lord underscored the importance of developing a disposition to do good continually when He declared, "I, the Lord, will not lay any sin to your charge; go your ways and sin no more; but unto that soul who sinneth shall the former sins return, saith the Lord your God" (D&C 82:7).

After the unrighteous Saul of Tarsus beheld a blinding heavenly light and heard the voice of Jesus Christ, he dramatically transformed his life and changed his name to Paul.

Following a period of temporary blindness, his sight was restored by a blessing at the hand of Ananias. The chronicler of Acts then recorded that "straightway he preached Christ in the synagogues, that he is the Son of God" (Acts 9:20). But Paul's first-person account of his conversion is more detailed than the version in Acts. Paul wrote the Galatians that after his conversion he did not immediately join the apostles in Jerusalem; rather, he "went into Arabia, and returned again unto Damascus. Then after three years, I went up to Jerusalem to see Peter, and abode with him fifteen days" (Galatians 1:17–18).

Despite Paul's teaching the gospel in Damascus, his brethren in Jerusalem "were all afraid of him, and believed not that he was a disciple" (Acts 9:26). Because of his reputation for having sought to destroy the Church, Paul had to "do good continually" for three years before others acknowledged that he had developed the disposition of a disciple of Christ.

MANIFESTATIONS OF DISPOSITIONS

We may manifest our disposition toward either good or evil in many ways. For example, we may perceive ourselves to be kind and charitable, but our penchant toward telling ethnic jokes belies our compassion. We may think we are patient and long-suffering, but we exhibit symptoms of road rage when another driver suddenly cuts in front of us. We may be compassionate and tolerant among work associates and neighbors, but we display unkindness and impatience with immediate family members.

Our use of time, especially leisure time, reveals our dispositions toward good and evil. The Lord declared, "For he who is faithful and wise in time is accounted worthy to inherit the mansions prepared for him of my Father" (D&C 72:4). Some individuals fill weekends and free evenings with television, whereas others visit the temple, read the scriptures and other great books, tutor school children, visit hospital patients, share the gospel with neighbors, work on family history, become involved in community improvement projects, and participate in countless other worthy activities. Theirs is the disposition to do good continually.

Our attitudes also reflect our dispositions toward good or evil. Chronic criticism, persistent pessimism, and their fellow travelers—sarcasm and cynicism—often reflect a lack of faith and trust in the Lord and a gnawing impatience for His great plan of happiness to unfold in our lives. Nephi strenuously admonished that we "must press forward with a steadfastness in Christ, having a perfect brightness of hope, and a love of God and of all men" (2 Nephi 31:20). In the final chapter of the Book of Mormon, Moroni reaffirmed that "there must be faith; and if there must be faith there must also be hope; and if there must be hope there must also be charity" (Moroni 10:20). He further taught that faith, hope, and charity are essential for salvation in the kingdom of God (Moroni 10:21).

Moroni then made a very important diagnostic declaration: "If ye have no hope ye must needs be in despair; and despair cometh because of iniquity" (Moroni 10:22). Moroni did *not* say despair occurs because of adversity. Countless individuals with pockmarked souls have been tested to the limit, but they remain faithful and steadfast. It is iniquity that begets despair because iniquity alienates the Comforter, who is a great source of faith and hope.

We manifest despair through a lack of faith, an absence of hope, and a failure to practice charity toward those who may have offended us or tried to destroy our dreams. Without the healing intervention of faith, hope, and charity, disappointment soon turns to grief and then to despair. President Boyd K. Packer reassures us that "it was meant to be that life would be a challenge. To suffer some anxiety, some depression, some disappointment, even some failure is normal."

He counsels us, "Teach our members that if they have a good, miserable day once in a while, or several in a row, to stand steady and face them. Things will straighten out. There is great purpose in our struggle in life."[3] As long as we practice charity, live righteously, nourish our testimony and faith, and increase our trust and hope in a loving Heavenly Father, our disappointments will not turn to anguish, hopelessness, and despair.

DIVINE DISPOSITIONS

It is well to contrast our human dispositions with the divine disposition of Jesus Christ. During His earthly ministry, the Savior humbly acknowledged that "I do nothing of myself; but as my Father hath taught me. . . . For I do always those things that please him" (John 8:28–29). In the Garden of Gethsemane, in the depths of agony, He compliantly prayed: "Nevertheless not my will, but thine, be done," thus reflecting "the will of the Son being swallowed up in the will of the Father" (Luke 22:42; Mosiah 15:7).

After having been commanded to sacrifice his young son Isaac, Abraham demonstrated to the Lord and to his posterity that he had a disposition to do good continually as he "rose up early in the morning" to make necessary preparations (Genesis 22:1–3).

Abraham's great-grandson, Joseph, provided another impressive example of an undeviating disposition to elude evil and to do good continually. When his master's wife sought to seduce him, Joseph indignantly responded, "How then can I do this great wickedness, and sin against God?" And he fled from her presence (Genesis 39:7–12). Joseph had decided long before meeting Potiphar's wife that he would never offend God.

When the Prophet Joseph Smith recounted the events surrounding the First Vision and the subsequent appearance of the angel Moroni, he confessed that, on occasion, he had "displayed the weakness of youth, and the foibles of human nature." He hastened to add that "no one need suppose me guilty of any great or malignant sins. A disposition to commit such was never in my nature" (JS–H 1:28).

During Zion's Camp, the Prophet demonstrated his natural disposition to do good. In May 1834, he and his brethren were pitching their tents on the Illinois prairie when some of the brethren suddenly discovered three rattlesnakes and were about to kill them. The Prophet immediately intervened, saying: "Let them alone—don't hurt them! How will the serpent ever lose his venom, while the servants of God possess the same disposition, and continue to make war upon it? Men must become harmless, before the brute creation; and when men lose their vicious dispositions and cease to destroy the animal race, the lion and the lamb can dwell together, and the sucking child can play with the serpent in safety."[4] The Prophet Joseph Smith lived as he preached.

Such is the disposition engendered by the Savior's admonition: "Love your enemies, bless them that curse you, do good to them that hate you, and pray for them which despitefully use you, and persecute you. . . . For if ye forgive men their trespasses, your heavenly Father will also forgive you" (Matthew 5:44; 6:14).

The Prophet Joseph Smith described well our current prophet when he declared, "Love is one of the chief characteristics of Deity, and ought to be manifested by those who aspire to be the sons of God. A man filled with the love of God is not content with blessing his family alone, but ranges through the whole world, anxious to bless the whole human race."[5] President Gordon B. Hinckley's exhausting travel schedule demonstrates his divine disposition to do good continually by foregoing the comforts of home in order to bless the Saints throughout the earth.

THE DISPOSITION OF ALMOST ALL MEN

In modern revelation the Lord has forewarned us "that it is the nature and disposition of almost all men, as soon as they get a little authority, as they suppose, they will immediately begin to exercise unrighteous dominion" (D&C 121:39). I can detect unrighteous dominion more easily in others than I can in myself. I consider myself to be candid, resolute, and exacting whereas others may consider me to be unkind, intransigent, and unreasonable.

One of the great safeguards against a disposition toward unrighteous dominion is the presidency principle and the council system in the Church. When leaders humbly seek and listen to the counsel of others, and when family members counsel together, they can generally make decisions that will receive the ratifying approbation of the Lord (D&C 107:26–30).

Our disposition to do good or evil is often reflected in our interpretations of the commandments and our reactions to the counsel of our Church leaders. For example, some individuals seek to negotiate a very narrow definition of tithing but prefer a very broad interpretation of the Word of Wisdom. In the words of President Marion G. Romney, "There are those among us who are trying to serve the Lord without offending the devil."[6] The lives of many faithful Latter-day Saints, however, reflect the disposition of the Savior, who always sought to do those things that pleased His Father (John 8:29).

COVENANT KEEPERS

Ordinances are outward manifestations of private, binding covenants, promises that we will strive to do good continually.

It is in the ordinances of the priesthood that "the power of godliness is manifest . . . unto men in the flesh" (D&C 84:20–21).
Each time we participate in priesthood ordinances, the powers
from on high reach downward and draw us nearer to the
heavens. Those who partake of the sacrament with pure hearts,
who worthily participate in the ordinances of the temple, and
who faithfully keep their covenants require no lengthy instructions regarding modest dress, payment of generous fast offerings and tithing, and observance of the Word of Wisdom and
the Sabbath Day. They do not need constant reminders to share
the gospel with others, attend the temple frequently, conduct
family history research, or do their home teaching and visiting
teaching. Nor do they need nudges to visit the sick and to serve
those in need.

These faithful Saints keep the sacred covenants they made
in the house of the Lord, "having a determination to serve him
to the end, and truly manifest by their works that they have
received of the Spirit of Christ unto the remission of their sins"
(D&C 20:37). Covenant keepers "are willing to bear one
another's burdens" and "are willing to mourn with those that
mourn; yea and comfort those that stand in need of comfort,
and to stand as witnesses of God at all times and in all things,
and in all places" (Mosiah 18:8–9).

Covenant keepers live the law of consecration. Their time,
talents, and financial resources all belong to the Lord. Keeping
their covenants has caused them to develop a disposition to do
good continually, and they are "willing to take upon them the
name of [the] Son, and *always* remember him and keep his
commandments which he has given them" (D&C 20:77;
emphasis added). Keeping covenants qualifies them to claim
the promised blessing of the sacramental prayer that "they may
always have [Christ's] Spirit to be with them" (D&C 20:77),

which helps them cultivate a disposition to do good continually and retain a remission of their sins.

NOTES

1. Smith, *Way to Perfection,* 150.
2. Talmage, *Jesus the Christ,* 126.
3. Packer, *That All May Be Edified,* 94.
4. Smith, *History of the Church,* 2:71.
5. Smith, *Teachings,* 174.
6. Romney, *The Price of Peace,* 7.

SIX

Abinadi's Song of Intercession

And thus God breaketh the bands of death, having gained the victory over death; giving the Son power to make intercession for the children of men—having ascended into heaven, having the bowels of mercy; being filled with compassion towards the children of men; standing betwixt them and justice (Mosiah 15:8–9).

You can count the seeds in an apple, but how many apples are in each seed? As the Restoration began to unfold, the Lord's influence in the affairs of His children became evident. A loving Heavenly Father will never override our moral agency and our freedom to choose; however, He does bring us within a certain circle of influence wherein we meet certain people. Afterward, our lives are never the same again.

Mendon is a village in upstate New York not far from Palmyra. The junction of the Mendon–Ionia Road and the Boughton Hill Road is called Tomlinson's Corners and is the location of the old Tomlinson Inn. In the spring of 1830, the Prophet Joseph Smith called his younger brother, Samuel, on a mission. In April of that year young Samuel made a stop at the

Tomlinson Inn to distribute copies of the newly published Book of Mormon to anyone who showed interest. On the same day Samuel visited the inn, an itinerant preacher named Phinehas Young stopped for dinner at the inn on his way home from Lima, where he had been preaching.

As Young was seated at the dinner table in conversation with others, Samuel approached him with a book in hand, saying, "There is a book, sir, I wish you to read." When Phinehas asked for a little background on the book, Samuel identified it as the Book of Mormon or the so-called Golden Bible. "Ah, sir, then it purports to be a revelation," Phinehas replied. "Yes," said Samuel, "it is a revelation from God. If you will read this book with a prayerful heart, and ask God to give you a witness, you will know of the truth of this work."

Phinehas promised Samuel he would do so, and before he left, Samuel testified, "I know the book to be a revelation from God, translated by the gift and power of the Holy Ghost, and that my brother Joseph Smith, Jun., is a Prophet, Seer and Revelator."[1]

After finishing his dinner, Phinehas went home and informed his wife, "I had got a week's work laid out," referring to his intention to read the Book of Mormon without major interruptions. Phinehas indicated that his intent was to "read it and make myself acquainted with its errors, so that I can expose them to the world." Like so many other self-styled critics whose intent is to discredit the Book of Mormon, Phinehas read the book through once and could find no errors. Upon reading it a second time he "felt a conviction that the book was true."

The following Sunday morning, Phinehas began preaching from the Book of Mormon and cited biblical scriptures that supported its divine purpose. He felt a great manifestation of the Spirit and concluded his sermon by testifying to the truthfulness of the Book of Mormon, observing, "The greater part of the people agreed with my views, and some of them said they had never heard me speak so well and with such power." He gave the book to his father, who read it and declared that "it was the greatest work and the clearest of error of anything he had ever seen, the Bible not excepted."[2]

We can well imagine that Samuel Smith may have returned to his home in Palmyra and reported to Joseph that his first attempts at placing copies of the Book of Mormon were modest at best, and that the reception he received was somewhat cool and indifferent. But Phinehas Young had some brothers—Brigham, John, and Joseph—who lived within a short stone's throw of Tomlinson Inn. The brothers Young had a close neighbor named Heber C. Kimball. Within months, a strong branch of the Church in Mendon had grown to about thirty members, including "ten Youngs, two Kimballs, the John P. Greene family, and even the owner of Tomlinson's Inn," which became the branch's meeting place.[3]

In April 1836, after the Church headquarters had been moved to Kirtland, Ohio, Parley P. Pratt was called on a mission to Toronto, Canada. It was there that he met John Taylor, who, in turn, introduced Parley to his good friend Joseph Fielding. John and his wife, Leonora, were baptized May 9, and Joseph and his sisters, Mary and Mercy, were baptized twelve days later.

After joining the main body of Saints in Kirtland, Joseph Fielding was eager to share the gospel with his relatives in England. Eventually, he, Heber C. Kimball, Orson Hyde, Willard Richards, John Goodson, Isaac Russell, and John Snider were called as the first missionaries to serve in the British Isles, arriving in Liverpool on July 19, 1837. Because Joseph Fielding's brother, James, was a preacher in Preston, the missionaries started their labors in that city. Joseph preached to his brother's congregation four days after the group's arrival. Within a week, nine members of the congregation had been baptized. James quickly withdrew his permission to allow the missionaries access to his congregation, vociferously complaining, "Kimball bored the holes, Goodson drove the nails, and Hyde clinched them."[4]

Elder Kimball continued preaching in the small villages of Downham, Chatburn, and Clitheroe, sometimes teaching the gospel in tithing barns, where commodities contributed by humble farmers to their churches were kept for distribution to the poor. Many villagers joined the Church, and by the conclusion of his mission, Heber C. Kimball had brought an estimated one thousand eight hundred souls into the Church. It all began with seeds planted by a testimony of the Book of Mormon.

ABINADI PLANTS A SEED

When we contemplate the impact of Abinadi's life and teachings in the Book of Mormon, we are again prompted to reflect upon the question: How many apples are in each seed? Abinadi's recorded time on the stage of the Book of Mormon was limited to about two years and only seven chapters, but let us consider the impact of his teachings. Because he taught by the power of the Spirit, the Spirit carried his words into the heart of one of wicked King Noah's priests named Alma. Alma believed all of Abinadi's words, and he became Abinadi's advocate before King Noah. But Alma soon realized that in pleading for Abinadi's life, he had himself become a life-threatened minority. He fled the king's court and recorded in detail all that he could remember of Abinadi's teaching (Mosiah 17:2–4).

Because of Alma's diligence in preaching the gospel and because of his devoted prayers in behalf of his wayward son, an angel appeared to Alma the Younger. That dramatic appearance changed not only the life of Alma the Younger but also the lives of his four friends, Ammon, Aaron, Omner, and Himni. As a result, all five of them went on missions to the Lamanites, during which Ammon gained the trust of King Lamoni through his disarming ability as a sheepherder.

After Lamoni's conversion, his father eventually gained an interest in the gospel and sent a proclamation throughout the land encouraging all his subjects to listen to the missionaries' message. Before his death, he relinquished his kingdom to his son, Anti-Nephi-Lehi. He, in turn, presided over thousands of newly converted Lamanites who wished to be called Anti-Nephi-Lehies to distinguish themselves from the Lamanites who were not converted.

Ultimately, the conversion of these thousands, who never did turn away from the church, can be traced directly to the seeds sown by Abinadi.

King Noah's father, Zeniff, had been a good man, albeit somewhat overzealous in seeking to reclaim lost lands from which the Nephites had been disinherited. His son, however, had led his subjects into apostasy. When Abinadi began preaching to the people, he prophesied that the king and his subjects would be destroyed if they did not repent. This bold approach soon landed him in prison and prompted King Noah to counsel with his priests regarding the fate of this man who had made all of them very uncomfortable. As the priests began to interrogate Abinadi regarding the meaning of various passages of scripture, their fragile questions readily disclosed the degree of their apostasy. Abinadi quickly accused them of pretending "to teach this people, and to understand the spirit of prophesying," adding, "Ye have not applied your hearts to understanding; therefore, ye have not been wise" (Mosiah 12:25, 27). After chastening the priests, he taught them the song of redeeming love:

"I say unto you, that salvation doth not come by the law alone; and were it not for the atonement, which God himself shall make for the sins and iniquities of his people, that they must unavoidably perish, notwithstanding the law of Moses.

"And now I say unto you that it was expedient that there should be a law given to the children of Israel, yea, even a very strict law; for they were a stiffnecked people, quick to do iniquity, and slow to remember the Lord their God;

"Therefore there was a law given them, yea, a law of performances and of ordinances, a law which they were to observe strictly from day to day, to keep them in remembrance of God and their duty towards him. But behold, I say unto you, that all these things were types of things to come.

"And now, did they understand the law? I say unto you, Nay, they did not all understand the law; and this because of the hardness of their hearts; for they understood not that there could not any man be saved except it were through the redemption of God" (Mosiah 13:28–32).

Like many ancient Israelites in the eastern hemisphere, the priests in King Noah's court had apparently observed the law of Moses in such a manner that they had, in Jacob's words, looked "beyond the mark" (Jacob 4:14). Abinadi reminded them that the rites and rituals of the law were "as a type . . . of things to come" (Mosiah 13:10) and were a means to an end, not an end in and of themselves. He then continued teaching the priests in the interrogative mode:

"For behold, did not Moses prophesy unto them concerning the coming of the Messiah, and that God should redeem his people? Yea, and even all the prophets who have prophesied ever since the world began—have they not spoken more or less concerning these things? Have they not said that God himself should come down among the children of men, and take upon him the form of man, and go forth in mighty power upon the face of the earth? Yea, and have they not said also that he should bring to pass the resurrection of the dead, and that he, himself, should be oppressed and afflicted?" (Mosiah 13:33–35).

After carefully reviewing in detail the implications of the law of Moses, Abinadi quoted one of Isaiah's messianic prophesies regarding Christ's atonement. Christ, he said, would be "a man of sorrows, and acquainted with grief," a man who "has borne our griefs, and carried our sorrows" (Mosiah 14:3–4; Isaiah 53:3–4). Abinadi, quoting Isaiah, testified that Christ "was wounded for our transgressions, he was bruised for our iniquities . . . and with his stripes we are healed" (Mosiah 14:5; Isaiah 53:5). And then, in supernal poignancy, he described the ultimate atoning sacrifice in which Christ "hath poured out his soul unto death . . . and made intercession for the transgressors . . . the will of the Son being swallowed up in the will of the Father" (Mosiah 14:12; 15:7).

"And thus God breaketh the bands of death, having gained the victory over death; giving the Son power to make intercession for the children of men—

"Having ascended into heaven, having the bowels of mercy, being filled with compassion towards the children of men; standing betwixt them and justice; having broken the bands of death, taken upon himself their iniquity and their transgressions, having redeemed them, and satisfied the demands of justice.

"And now I say unto you, who shall declare his generation? Behold, I say unto you, that when his soul has been made an offering for sin he shall see his seed. And now what say ye? And who shall be his seed?

"Behold I say unto you, that whosoever has heard the words of the prophets, yea, all the holy prophets who have prophesied concerning the coming of the Lord—I say unto you, that all those who have hearkened unto their words, and believed that the Lord would redeem his people, and have looked forward to that day for a remission of their sins, I say unto you, that these are his seed, or they are the heirs of the kingdom of God" (Mosiah 15:8–11).

At the conclusion of King Benjamin's benedictory sermon, after his followers had undergone a mighty change of heart, he explained that "because of the covenant which ye have made ye shall be called the children of Christ, his sons, and his daughters" (Mosiah 5:7). Abinadi reaffirmed this principle, adding that the seed of Christ are those who have "heard the words of the prophets" and have "hearkened unto their words, and believed that the Lord would redeem his people, and have looked forward to that day for a remission of their sins" (Mosiah 15:11).

When John the Baptist began his mission to prepare the way of the Lord, he met great resistance among those who claimed to be direct descendants of Abraham and who assumed that their salvation was secure by virtue of their genealogy. Like King Benjamin and Abinadi, he urged the people to "bring forth therefore fruits meet for repentance." Then, to really get to the heart of the matter, he said, "And think not to say within yourselves, We have Abraham to our father: for I say unto you, that God is able of these stones to raise up children unto Abraham" (Matthew 3:8–9).

It is wonderful to claim a rich heritage and to be able to count a large number of pioneer progenitors. But King Benjamin, Abinadi, and John intimate that it is just as desirable to be a pioneer convert to the Church.

During more than a decade of living in Europe, we have had the blessing of meeting missionaries from Albania, Bulgaria, the Czech Republic, Hungary, Russia, Mongolia, and many other lands. These missionaries are their respective nations' Heber C. Kimballs and Parley P. Pratts. Though many of them have been members of the Church only a year or so, were not deacons for two years, did not graduate from seminary, and did not experience family home evening in their youth, they will be able to claim the Savior's promise that if they remain faithful, "all that my father hath shall be given unto [them]" (D&C 84:38).

"O how beautiful upon the mountains are the feet of him that bringeth good tidings, that is the founder of peace, yea, even the Lord, who has redeemed his people; yea, him who has granted salvation unto his people;

"For were it not for the redemption which he hath made for his people, which was prepared from the foundation of the world, I say unto you, were it not for this, all mankind must have perished.

"But behold, the bands of death shall be broken, and the Son reigneth, and hath power over the dead; therefore, he bringeth to pass the resurrection of the dead. And there cometh a resurrection, even a first resurrection; yea, even a resurrection of those that have been, and who are, and who shall be, even until the resurrection of Christ—for so shall he be called.

"And now, the resurrection of all the prophets, and all those that have believed in their words, or all those that have kept the commandments of God, shall come forth in the first resurrection; therefore, they are the first resurrection. They are raised to dwell with God who has redeemed them; thus they have eternal life through Christ, who has broken the bands of death.

"And these are those who have part in the first resurrection; and these are they that have died before Christ came, in their ignorance, not having salvation declared unto them. And thus the Lord bringeth about the restoration of these; and they have a part in the first resurrection, or have eternal life, being redeemed by the Lord. And little children also have eternal life" (Mosiah 15:18–25).

Just as the Israelites looked beyond the mark regarding the importance and purpose of the law of Moses, so some denominations have looked beyond the Savior's statement to Nicodemus that "except a man be born of the water and of the Spirit, he cannot enter into the kingdom of God" (John 3:5). The misunderstanding of this commandment, coupled with confusion that children are born into the world in a degenerate state because of the original sin of Adam and Eve, has caused considerable anguish to the parents of young babes who have died in infancy.

One of the internal evidences of the divine origins of the Book of Mormon is the clarification of the false, disheartening doctrine that unbaptized children are condemned to purgatory. Abinadi and King Benjamin countermand that false assumption early in the first half of the Book of Mormon (Mosiah 3:18–19; 15:25), and Mormon explains in greater detail in the book's second half that "little children cannot repent; wherefore, it is awful wickedness to deny the pure mercies of God unto them, for they are alive in him because of his mercy. And he that saith that little children need baptism denieth the mercies of Christ, and setteth at naught the atonement of him and the power of his redemption" (Moroni 8:19).

On the other hand, Abinadi discharges his duty well in warning the priests of King Noah and others beyond the age of accountability who have sinned:

"But behold, and fear, and tremble before God, for ye ought to tremble; for the Lord redeemeth none such that rebel against him and die in their sins; yea, even all those that have perished in their sins ever since the world began, that have wilfully rebelled against God, that have known the commandments of God, and would not keep them; these are they that have no part in the first resurrection.

"Therefore ought ye not to tremble? For salvation cometh to none such; for the Lord hath redeemed none such; yea, neither can the Lord redeem such; for he cannot deny himself; for he cannot deny justice when it has its claim" (Mosiah 15:26–27).

"And now if Christ had not come into the world, *speaking of things to come as though they had already come*, there could have been no redemption. . . . Teach [the people] that redemption cometh through Christ the Lord, who is the very Eternal Father. Amen" (Mosiah 16:6, 15; emphasis added).

INTERCESSION OF A HOME TEACHER

Kenneth Boyd was a pleasure boat proprietor who had an enjoyable lifestyle providing the jet-set crowd from big cities in the North with a relaxing vacation around the Caribbean. Such vacations generally involved a good deal of drinking, and Ken was a gracious host. One day, when he was in his mid-fifties, Ken went to see his doctor because he had not been feeling well. After a series of tests, the physician suggested that he retire to preserve his health.

"But I'm not old enough to retire," he protested. "*You* may not be," rejoined the doctor, "but your *liver* is. If you don't stop drinking, you will have only six months to live."

Ken took the warning to heart, quit drinking, sold his business, and moved to the Carolinas. One day two young men knocked on his door and asked if he had time to hear a brief message. Ken responded, "My doctor tells me I have six months." As Ken and his wife listened to the missionary discussions, their hearts were touched, and not long after they were baptized, they felt impressed to move to Idaho.

Shortly after their arrival in their new ward, Bishop John Olsen called Kenneth into his office to give him a special assignment. Members of the bishopric were concerned about the Durrant family, and they felt that Kenneth Boyd, as a recent convert, might be able to reach them and influence their lives. As Kenneth accepted the assignment to visit this family, the bishop added one bit of counsel: "The Durrants have two large dogs, a rottweiler and a German shepherd. You may want to be careful the first visit or two." Brother Boyd had been told that he might have only six months to live, but being devoured by two watchdogs was not the way he intended to go.

The doctor had told Kenneth that a brisk daily walk would be good for his health, so each morning he got up before the sun and walked to the Durrants' home while they were still asleep. When the guard dogs would run to the front fence to see who was invading their territory, Kenneth would throw them scraps of food over the fence. Each evening he would save a little strip of fat, chicken skin, or crust of bread to take to the Durrants' dogs the next morning. He repeated this ritual each morning for several weeks.

Kenneth then asked to meet again with the bishop and requested help in researching the Durrants' family history. After the bishop explained how such information could be procured from the family history center, Kenneth began tracing the family roots of the Durrants, including biographical sketches of various ancestors. At last he was ready to make his first visit. He gave the Durrants a call and set up an appointment. "You can come if you're brave enough," Brother Durrant responded without much warmth.

At the appointed hour, Kenneth appeared at the Durrants' front gate. The rottweiler surged toward him from one side of the house while the German shepherd charged from the other side. Brother Durrant heard the barking and came to the front porch expecting to see a massacre. Instead, the two guard dogs began licking the back of the hand of the kindly benefactor who had been feeding them scraps for several weeks. Absolutely astounded, Brother Durrant invited Brother Boyd to come in.

Kenneth began the visit by asking the Durrants what they knew about their ancestors from England. They had some

vague childhood recollections of accounts about early ancestors who joined the Church in the Old Country and traveled
to Zion by ship. But somewhere along the way, testimonies and
Church activity began to wane, and the current generation had
little to do with the faith of their fathers.

Brother Boyd began telling the Durrants what he had
learned about their ancestors, and, as he did so, the spirit of
family history work began to melt icy hearts and turn them
toward their long-forgotten fathers and mothers of previous generations. The Durrants were fascinated with all they heard, and
when Kenneth suggested it was time for him to leave, they
begged him to stay. They felt an unusually peaceful spirit in their
home, and they wanted to keep it as long as they could. Kenneth
said he would return the same time the following week.

A week later the Durrants invited their married children to
come to meet Brother Boyd. Soon he was teaching many in the
extended family. Hearts were softened toward the gospel and,
with the passage of time, many members of the Durrant family
were sealed in the Idaho Falls Temple.

When Kenneth Boyd joined the Church, he learned the
song of redeeming love. Having once learned that song, he felt
an unrelenting obligation to intercede in the lives of others to
share the wondrous song he loved so well.

NOTES

1. *Millennial Star,* 25:360–61.
2. *Millennial Star,* 25:361.
3. Kimball, *Heber C. Kimball,* 19.
4. Bloxham, *Truth Will Prevail,* 76.

SEVEN

Alma the Elder's Song of Deliverance

And it came to pass that the voice of the Lord came to them in their afflictions, saying: Lift up your heads and be of good comfort, for I know of the covenant which ye have made unto me; and I will covenant with my people and deliver them out of bondage (Mosiah 24:13).

The great Jehovah and Savior of the world has many titles and is described by many terms of adoration. One of these is the Great Deliverer. The bondage suffered by the children of Israel in Egypt was often referred to by subsequent prophets as a type and shadow of spiritual bondage to sin. Just as Jehovah of the Old Testament liberated the Israelites from bondage in Egypt, so Jesus Christ of the New Testament can liberate us from the bondage of sin.

Throughout the Book of Mormon, various groups suffered subjugation. Book of Mormon prophets likened their physical bondage to spiritual bondage, from which deliverance was only possible through the atoning sacrifice of Jesus Christ and upon conditions of personal repentance.

After Alma the Elder heard the words of Abinadi, his life

was never the same. He tried to protect Abinadi from death, but in doing so Alma endangered his own life and had to flee. Upon repenting of his iniquities, Alma "went about privately among the people, and began to teach the words of Abinadi" concerning Christ's coming redemption, resurrection, and ascension (Mosiah 18:1–2). Soon a substantial group of new converts gathered at a place called Mormon. There they "came to the knowledge of their Redeemer; yea, and how blessed are they, for they shall sing to his praise forever" (Mosiah 18:30).

In that inspiring natural setting, Alma taught his followers, or rather the followers of Christ, the requirements of the baptismal covenant they were preparing to make. Membership in Christ's church requires us to "mourn with those that mourn; yea, and comfort those that stand in need of comfort, and . . . stand as witnesses of God at all times and in all things, and in all places" and to "serve him and keep his commandments" (Mosiah 18:9–10).

The four hundred and fifty souls who entered into the baptismal covenant at the waters of Mormon were so fond of Alma that they later asked him to become their king. He declined the honor, agreeing instead to serve as their presiding high priest.

As soon as the Lord's Church begins to grow, so does concomitant persecution. Fearing that Alma's faithful followers would become a source of sedition, King Noah commanded his army to destroy them. They fled for their lives to a land they named Helam, but no sooner had they escaped from the clutches of the king than they were encircled by Lamanites. Fortunately, "the Lord did soften the hearts of the Lamanites," and the believers were spared (Mosiah 18:33–35; 23:6–16, 25–29).

The king of the Lamanites selected Amulon, one of King Noah's wicked priests, to become his puppet ruler over the Nephites. Amulon's authoritarian leadership was so repressive that he even forbade Alma's people from praying aloud upon penalty of death. Nevertheless, the people "did pour out their hearts to [God]; and he did know the thoughts of their hearts." The Lord's voice spoke comfort to their souls, that as they had covenanted with Him, so He would covenant to "deliver them out of bondage." He also promised to "ease the burdens which are put upon your shoulders, that even you cannot feel them upon your backs." And "the burdens which were laid upon Alma and his brethren were made light . . . and they did submit cheerfully and with patience to all the will of the Lord" (Mosiah 24:12–15).

It seems significant that the Lord did not remove their burdens; rather, He eased and lightened their burdens. Bearing burdens, like exercising our physical muscles, strengthens our spirituality, faith, and trust in the Lord. A life without burdens readily becomes a life of boredom, devoid of meaning and purpose. But, as the apostle Paul assures us, "God is faithful, who will not suffer you to be tempted above that ye are able; but will with the temptation [or burden] also make a way to escape, that ye may be able to bear it" (1 Corinthians 10:13).

The Lord caused a deep sleep to fall upon the Lamanites, allowing Alma and his people to escape into the wilderness. Arriving at a place they called the valley of Alma, "they poured out their thanks to God because he had been merciful unto them, and eased their burdens, and had delivered them out of bondage; for they were in bondage, and none could deliver them except it were the Lord their God" (Mosiah 24:19–21).

In response to Alma's faithfulness, the Lord gave him an extraordinary promise: "Thou art my servant; and I covenant with thee that thou shalt have eternal life; and thou shalt serve me and go forth in my name, and shalt gather together my sheep. And he that will hear my voice shall be my sheep; and him shall ye receive into the church, and him will I also receive.

"For behold, this is my church; whosoever is baptized shall be baptized unto repentance. And whomsoever ye receive shall believe in my name; and him will I freely forgive. For it is I that taketh upon me the sins of the world; for it is I that hath created them; and it is I that granteth unto him that believeth unto the end a place at my right hand.

"For behold, in my name are they called; and if they know me they shall come forth, and shall have a place eternally at my right hand. And it shall come to pass that when the second trump shall sound then shall they that never knew me come forth and shall stand before me. And then shall they know that I am the Lord their God, that I am their Redeemer; but they would not be redeemed. And then I will confess unto them that I never knew them; and they shall depart into everlasting fire prepared for the devil and his angels.

"Therefore I say unto you, that he that will not hear my voice, the same shall ye not receive into my church, for him I will not receive at the last day. Therefore I say unto you, Go; and whosoever transgresseth against me, him shall ye judge according to the sins which he has committed; and if he confess his sins before thee and me, and repenteth in the sincerity of his heart, him shall ye forgive, and I will forgive him also.

"Yea, and as often as my people repent will I forgive them their trespasses against me. And ye shall also forgive one another your trespasses; for verily I say unto you, he that forgiveth not his neighbor's trespasses when he says that he repents, the same hath brought himself under condemnation.

"Now I say unto you, Go; and whosoever will not repent of his sins the same shall not be numbered among my people; and this shall be observed from this time forward" (Mosiah 26:20–32).

Many of us are in bondage for one reason or another throughout our lives. Sometimes we are in bondage to sin, sometimes to a physical or emotional condition, or sometimes to financial circumstances. When we pay off our house, car, and credit card, we are free from financial bondage. When we fully repent of our sins, though we will ever be indebted to the Great Deliverer, we are free from spiritual bondage! The Great Deliverer, in turn, expects us to deliver others from bondage.

TEMPORING JUSTICE

Few individuals have understood that better than Sister Annaroesli Biersfelder. This Swiss sister, as saintly a woman as ever lived, recently passed away. Annaroesli was a lovely young woman when she joined the Church with her husband, Georg. Shortly after their marriage, the mission president asked Georg if he was ready to serve a mission. Though struggling financially, as most young couples do, they arranged their affairs so that Annaroesli would work to support her husband on his mission.

They waited in great anticipation for a letter announcing Georg's call, but their waiting was in vain. When the mission president finally revisited their little branch, Georg mustered the courage to ask him about his mission. "Oh," replied the jovial mission president, slapping Georg on the back, "I was only joking with you, Georg. You and Annaroesli have another important mission—to raise a family."

Both Georg and Annaroesli were crestfallen, but the mission president was right. They needed to rear a righteous family, and that they did. But they always harbored a dream of serving a mission.

We first met Elder and Sister Biersfelder more than a dozen years ago while they were serving a mission in the Freiberg Germany Temple. We met again a few years later while they were serving in the Frankfurt Germany Temple.

After completing their temple assignment one day, the

Biersfelders took a stroll along the little streets of Friedericksdorf, where the Frankfurt Temple is located. These narrow streets of brick and cobblestone have very short curbs. As the Biersfelders walked along the sidewalk, an elderly man turned a corner too widely, his car jumping the tiny curb and hitting Sister Biersfelder from behind. Thrust through a store's thick plate-glass door and knocked unconscious, she was rushed to the hospital. Once there, Sister Biersfelder was diagnosed as having a double skull fracture with a life-threatening concussion that left her comatose. She also lost the sight of one eye.

For seven long weeks, she lay comatose in her hospital bed. Her loving husband spent countless hours at her bedside, patting her hand and speaking soft words of encouragement. The entire Frankfurt Stake held a special fast on her behalf, uniting in faith and prayers that the Lord's will be done. Though we feared the worst, all of us were inspired by Brother Biersfelder's faith and ebullient optimism.

After the seemingly endless vigil, Sister Biersfelder one day opened her eyes. Two months after this traumatic accident, she began to speak again and, with assistance, to sit up in bed and eat. Ten weeks after the accident, we visited her in the hospital. She could stand, take a few steps, and speak to us in English, French, and German. She was a living miracle—our prayers had been answered.

Notwithstanding the impressive progress she had made, she still experienced considerable pain, including splitting headaches. One day she received a surprise visitor in the hospital—an elderly man whom Annaroesli did not recognize. With great anxiety, perhaps fearing legal reprisals, the man introduced himself as the driver of the car who had caused her such pain and suffering.

As he neared her bed, he asked her, "Do you hate me for what I have done to you?" Her response was totally unexpected. "Do you know who I am? I am a Latter-day Saint. In our religion we love one another. I am convinced that you didn't intentionally harm me. I don't hate you. I love you and forgive you."

That day the elderly man was delivered from his guilt and a great load upon his shoulders. He was so relieved that he met with the local Huguenot minister and told him of receiving Sister Biersfelder's forgiveness. The minister's heart was touched and he shared this experience with his congregation, extolling the virtues of Sister Biersfelder in extending forgiveness to the man who had been the source of great physical pain and anguish. Since then the relations between the Latter-day Saint temple patrons and the local Huguenot citizens have been excellent, thanks to Sister Biersfelder's magnanimous heart.

After serving as a counselor in the Freiberg, Frankfurt, and Swiss Temples, Brother Biersfelder was called to be the president of the Swiss Temple, where his lovely wife stood beside him as the temple matron. Though she filled her responsibilities cheerfully under a cloud of pain, Sister Biersfelder assisted her husband in extending a warm and gentle welcome to all who entered the house of the Lord.

Not long after President Biersfelder was released as temple president, his eternal companion passed on to her eternal reward. She was graciously delivered from constant pain even as she had graciously delivered the perpetrator of her troubles from the pain of guilt and remorse. She could claim the Lord's promise that "when he shall appear we shall be like him . . . purified even as he is pure" (Moroni 7:48).

EIGHT

Alma the Younger's Song of Being Snatched from Sin

Nevertheless, after wading through much tribulation, repenting nigh unto death, the Lord in mercy hath seen fit to snatch me out of an everlasting burning, and I am born of God. . . . My soul was racked with eternal torment; but I am snatched, and my soul is pained no more (Mosiah 27:28–29).

Many years ago I attended a memorable priesthood meeting in which the lesson centered on the Atonement. Our teacher was an elderly man in his mid-seventies with thinning strands of pure white hair. He had spent most of his life working with his hands. He was not especially articulate, nor could he be described as a master teacher. Yet the spirit of his lesson has remained with me for more than two decades because of the certitude of his testimony.

I learned some time later that our good teacher had been a model husband and father and had successfully supported and reared a rather large family. He emphasized the importance of good music in his home, and each of his children had brought honor to him and his wife by freely sharing their musical talents with others.

Decades prior to this memorable priesthood lesson, the teacher had allowed Satan to cloud his memory of the sacred temple covenants he had made. In an unguarded moment, he wasted his virtue on an unworthy woman. A disciplinary council was held, and he lost his membership in the Church, the privilege of holding the Melchizedek Priesthood, the blessing of the temple endowment, and his sealing to his wife and children.

His wife told him she would forgive him if he would fully repent, but she had no intention of following him to hell. This philandering husband understood her message. After he passed through a long period of agonizing remorse, his priesthood leaders felt that he was ready to be rebaptized. A year or two later he received all he had lost, and since that time he had served faithfully in every calling and had been a devout temple patron.

Now, after the passage of a quarter century, this good man was teaching his brethren from firsthand experience about the refreshing waters of baptism, the sweet return of the companionship of the Holy Spirit, and the miracle of forgiveness. The pedagogy was simple and straightforward, devoid of theatrical embellishment. He simply knew that the Atonement was infinite and comprehensive and that it included him. He never once referred to his own painful experience, but he could not refrain from tears when he discussed the suffering of the Savior in the Garden of Gethsemane and upon the cross at Golgotha.

He had gained a small taste of Christ's ordeal by suffering for his own sins, and he could only imagine how great the suffering would be to heap everyone's sins upon the Savior's bleeding back and shoulders. When he testified of the truth of the Atonement, though he did not fully understand how the cleansing actually occurs, he testified that the purification process is real and available to all. Because the Spirit testified to our hearts that what he said was true, we knew that he had been forgiven, and we felt certain that we could be forgiven.

Our venerable teacher's euphoria and gratitude were similar to the feelings Alma the Younger expressed following the appearance of an angel who told Alma he had "come to convince [him] of the power and authority of God, that the prayers of his servants might be answered according to their faith" (Mosiah 27:14). Alma fell to the earth, became dumb, and lost the use of his limbs. After Church leaders had fasted and prayed for two days, Alma regained his voice and physical strength and stood before the people, exclaiming:

"I have repented of my sins, and have been redeemed of the Lord; behold I am born of the Spirit. And the Lord said unto me: Marvel not that all mankind, yea, men and women, all nations, kindreds, tongues and people, must be born again; yea, born of God, changed from their carnal and fallen state, to a state of righteousness, being redeemed of God, becoming his sons and daughters;

"And thus they become new creatures; and unless they do this, they can in nowise inherit the kingdom of God. I say unto you, unless this be the case, they must be cast off; and this I know, because I was like to be cast off.

"Nevertheless, after wading through much tribulation, repenting nigh unto death, the Lord in mercy hath seen fit to snatch me out of an everlasting burning, and I am born of God.

"My soul hath been redeemed from the gall of bitterness and bonds of iniquity. I was in the darkest abyss; but now I behold the marvelous light of God. My soul was racked with eternal torment; but I am snatched, and my soul is pained no more.

"I rejected my Redeemer, and denied that which had been

spoken of by our fathers; but now that they may foresee that he will come, and that he remembereth every creature of his creating, he will make himself manifest unto all" (Mosiah 27:24–30).

Decades later, Alma recounted the visitation of the angel while counseling his son Helaman. Though several years had passed, Alma recalled the agony and ecstasy in great detail:

"For I went about with the sons of Mosiah, seeking to destroy the church of God; but behold, God sent his holy angel to stop us by the way. . . . And he said unto me: If thou wilt of thyself be destroyed, seek no more to destroy the church of God. . . .

"And now, for three days and for three nights was I racked, even with the pains of a damned soul. And it came to pass that as I was thus racked with torment, while I was harrowed up by the memory of my many sins, behold, I remembered also to have heard my father prophesy unto the people concerning the coming of one Jesus Christ, a Son of God, to atone for the sins of the world.

"Now, as my mind caught hold upon this thought, I cried within my heart: O Jesus, thou Son of God, have mercy on me, who am in the gall of bitterness, and am encircled about by the everlasting chains of death.

"And now, behold, when I thought this, I could remember my pains no more; yea, I was harrowed up by the memory of my sins no more. And oh, what joy, and what marvelous light I did behold; yea, my soul was filled with joy as exceeding as was my pain!

"Yea, I say unto you, my son, that *there could be nothing so exquisite and so bitter as were my pains*. Yea, and again I say unto you, my son, that on the other hand, *there can be nothing so exquisite and sweet as was my joy*" (Alma 36:6, 9, 16–21; emphasis added).

After his-dramatic conversion, Alma spent the rest of his life teaching the song of redeeming love, testifying with certainty of a Savior who would come to earth:

"For behold, I say unto you there be many things to come; and behold, there is one thing which is of more importance than they all—for behold, the time is not far distant that the Redeemer liveth and cometh among his people. . . .

"And behold, he shall be born of Mary, at Jerusalem which is the land of our forefathers, she being a virgin, a precious and chosen vessel, who shall be overshadowed and conceive by the power of the Holy Ghost, and bring forth a son, yea, even the Son of God.

"And he shall go forth, suffering pains and afflictions and temptations of every kind; and this that the word might be fulfilled which saith he will take upon him the pains and the sicknesses of his people.

"And he will take upon him death, that he may loose the bands of death which bind his people; and he will take upon him their infirmities, that his bowels may be filled with mercy, according to the flesh, that he may know according to the flesh how to succor his people according to their infirmities" (Alma 7:7, 10–12).

These latter two verses provide valuable insight into the Savior's infinite Atonement. Elsewhere we learn of His intense suffering for our sins, but it is Alma who informs us that His suffering also includes cancer, arthritis, multiple sclerosis, depression, broken hearts, unfulfilled dreams, and all other infirmities of the flesh. Indeed, His atoning sacrifice includes His promise: "I will not leave you comfortless" (John 14:18.) A latter-day corollary is the promise that "thine adversity and thine afflictions shall be but a small moment; and then, if thou endure it well, God shall exalt thee on high," and He shall "consecrate thine afflictions for thy gain" (D&C 121:7–8; 2 Nephi 2:2). Pain is inevitable, but misery is optional.

Throughout the years, I have observed that self-pity in the midst of affliction can become like cataracts to our vision. It is sometimes difficult in the depths of despair to discern how a loving Heavenly Father can consecrate our afflictions for our gain. But when we count our blessings, search the scriptures, and lose ourselves in the service of others, our disappointments and despair diminish, our hearts become hopeful, our faith begins to flourish, and our Savior gives us comfort that passes human understanding.

Our tiny sips of suffering give us a greater appreciation for the Savior's not shrinking from drinking the bitter cup—all of it. Indeed, He "poured out his soul unto death" (Isaiah 53:12) in order to make room for *all* of the sins and guilt and suffering of the world.

The Savior's atonement may not immediately remove *all* our physical pain, but if our hearts are right and we refuse to wallow in self-pity, we will quite naturally reflect upon the intense pain the Savior suffered in Gethsemane and on Golgotha. We will be drawn closer to Him because we have more in common with Him, though our anguish and pain pale by comparison.

In the aftermath of three painful operations, Elder Robert D. Hales humbly disclosed that "in the past two years, I have waited upon the Lord for mortal lessons to be taught me through periods of physical pain, mental anguish, and pondering. I learned that constant, intense pain is a great consecrating purifier that humbles us and draws us closer to God's Spirit."[1]

President James E. Faust assures us that "out of the refiner's fire can come a glorious deliverance. It can be a noble and lasting rebirth. The price to become acquainted with God will have been paid. There can come a sacred peace. There will be a reawakening of dormant, inner resources. A comfortable cloak of righteousness will be drawn around us to protect us and to keep us warm spiritually. Self-pity will vanish as our blessings are counted."[2]

The greatest burden we have to bear is not physical, mental, or emotional infirmity but rather the burden of sin. Alma forthrightly proposed a solution to this burden:

"Now the Spirit knoweth all things; nevertheless the Son of God suffereth according to the flesh that he might take upon him the sins of his people, that he might blot out their transgressions according to the power of his deliverance; and now behold, this is the testimony which is in me.

"Now I say unto you that ye must repent, and be born again; for the Spirit saith if ye are not born again ye cannot inherit the kingdom of heaven; therefore come and be baptized unto repentance, that ye may be washed from your sins, that ye may have faith on the Lamb of God, who taketh away the sins of the world, who is mighty to save and to cleanse from all unrighteousness.

"Yea, I say unto you come and fear not, and lay aside every sin, which easily doth beset you, which doth bind you down to destruction, yea, come and go forth, and show unto your God that ye are willing to repent of your sins and enter into a covenant with him to keep his commandments, and witness it unto him this day by going into the waters of baptism.

"And whosoever doeth this, and keepeth the commandments of God from thenceforth, the same will remember that I say unto him, yea, he will remember that I have said unto him, he shall have eternal life, according to the testimony of the Holy Spirit, which testifieth in me" (Alma 7:13–16).

The Lord revealed to the Prophet Joseph Smith that "the Book of Mormon and the holy scriptures are given of me for your instruction; and *the power of my Spirit quickeneth all things*" (D&C 33:16; emphasis added). One of the common characteristics shared by servants of the Lord is a sense of spiritual urgency regarding the work in which they are engaged. Take Abraham, for example. Notwithstanding the heartstring-plucking poignancy of being commanded to sacrifice his son, "Abraham rose up *early* in the morning" to take Isaac to the appointed sacrificial altar on Mount Moriah (Genesis 22:3; emphasis added).

In the fields outside Bethlehem, after the shepherds had heard the angel's voice and the heavenly host praising God, "they came with *haste*, and found Mary, and Joseph, and the babe lying in a manger" (Luke 2:8–16; emphasis added).

After Alma had been reviled and cast out of the city of Ammonihah, an angel appeared to exhort him to return to the city. Obeying, "he returned *speedily* to the land of Ammonihah," where he met Amulek, who became his host and missionary companion (Alma 8:18–21; emphasis added). Together they began to warn the people with a great sense of urgency: "And not many days hence the Son of God shall come in his glory; and his glory shall be the glory of the Only Begotten of the Father, full of grace, equity, and truth, full of patience, mercy, and long-suffering, quick to hear the cries of his people and to answer their prayers. And behold, he cometh to redeem those who will be baptized unto repentance, through faith on his name" (Alma 9:26–27).

Early in their missionary labors, Alma and Amulek encountered a crafty lawyer named Zeezrom. Perhaps in response to Zeezrom's profession and rigorous legal training, Alma systematically unfolded the plan of redemption:

"Now, if it had not been for the plan of redemption, which was laid from the foundation of the world, there could have been no resurrection of the dead; but there was a plan of redemption laid, which shall bring to pass the resurrection of the dead, of which has been spoken.

"And now behold, if it were possible that our first parents could have gone forth and partaken of the tree of life they would have been forever miserable, having no preparatory state; and thus the plan of redemption would have been frustrated, and the word of God would have been void, taking none effect. . . .

"Therefore he sent angels to converse with them, who caused men to behold of his glory. And they began from that time forth to call on his name; therefore God conversed with men, and made known unto them the plan of redemption, which had been prepared from the foundation of the world; and this he made known unto them according to their faith and repentance and their holy works.

"Wherefore, he gave commandments unto men, they having first transgressed the first commandments as to things which were temporal, and becoming as Gods, knowing good from evil, placing themselves in a state to act, or being placed in a state to act according to their wills and pleasures, whether to do evil or to do good—

"Therefore *God gave unto them commandments, after having made known unto them the plan of redemption,* that they should not do evil, the penalty thereof being a second death, which was an everlasting death as to things pertaining unto righteousness; for on such the plan of redemption could have no power, for the works of justice could not be destroyed, according to the supreme goodness of God" (Alma 12:25–26, 29–32; emphasis added).

Jacob taught that "where there is no law given there is no punishment; and where there is no punishment there is no condemnation" (2 Nephi 9:25). Amplifying upon the relationship among law, sin, mercy, and justice, Alma taught his son, Corianton:

"And now, the plan of mercy could not be brought about except an atonement should be made; therefore God himself atoneth for the sins of the world, to bring about the plan of mercy, to appease the demands of justice, that God might be a perfect, just God, and a merciful God also.

"Now, repentance could not come unto men except there were a punishment, which also was eternal as the life of the soul should be, affixed opposite to the plan of happiness, which was as eternal also as the life of the soul.

"Now, how could a man repent except he should sin? How could he sin if there was no law? How could there be a law save there was a punishment? . . .

"But there is a law given, and a punishment affixed, and a repentance granted; which repentance, mercy claimeth; otherwise, justice claimeth the creature and executeth the law, and the law inflicteth the punishment; if not so, the works of justice would be destroyed, and God would cease to be God.

"But God ceaseth not to be God, and mercy claimeth the penitent, and mercy cometh because of the atonement; and the atonement bringeth to pass the resurrection of the dead; and the resurrection of the dead bringeth back men into the presence of God; and thus they are restored into his presence, to be judged according to their works, according to the law and justice.

"For behold, justice exerciseth all his demands, and also mercy claimeth all which is her own; and thus, none but the truly penitent are saved" (Alma 42:15–17, 22–24).

In the scriptures the Lord has given each of us a promised avenue whereby we may be forgiven of our sins. James explained that "he which converteth the sinner from the error of his way shall save a soul from death, and shall hide a multitude of sins" (James 5:20). And in latter-day revelation the Lord gives us an admonition with a promise: "Therefore, thrust in your sickle with all your soul, and your sins are forgiven you" (D&C 31:5). The Lord extends another promise: "For I will forgive you of your sins with this commandment—that you remain steadfast in your minds in solemnity and the spirit of prayer, in bearing testimony to all the world of those things which are communicated unto you" (D&C 84:61).

Alma exulted in the knowledge that he had been forgiven of his sins, and he could hardly contain the joy he felt in being the Lord's instrument in bringing other souls to repentance. Notwithstanding Alma's missionary success and the assurance he had received that he had been forgiven of his sins, his joy fell short of pomposity and pride.

"And behold, when I see many of my brethren truly penitent, and coming to the Lord their God, then is my soul filled with joy; then do I remember what the Lord has done for me, yea, even that he hath heard my prayer; yea, then do I remember his merciful arm which he extended towards me" (Alma 29:10).

SNATCHED FROM SIN

President Howard W. Hunter related the account of a young man who had quite literally been snatched from sin in a most remarkable way:

"As a young man, Brother Vern Crowley said he learned something of the crucial lesson the Prophet Joseph had taught the early Saints in Nauvoo when he told them to 'love others, even our enemies as well as friends.' This is a good lesson for each of us.

"After his father became ill, Vern Crowley took responsibility for running the family wrecking yard although he was only fifteen years of age. Some customers occasionally took unfair advantage of the young man, and parts were disappearing from the lot overnight. Vern was angry and vowed to catch someone and make an example of him. Vengeance would be his.

"Just after his father had started to recover from his illness, Vern was making his rounds of the yard one night at closing time. It was nearly dark. In a distant corner of the property, he caught sight of someone carrying a large piece of machinery toward the back fence. He ran like a champion athlete and caught the young thief. His first thought was to take out his frustrations with his fists and then drag the boy to the front office and call the police. His heart was full of anger and vengeance. He had caught his thief, and he intended to get his just dues.

"Out of nowhere, Vern's father came along, put his weak and infirm hand on his son's shoulder, and said, 'I see you're a bit upset, Vern. Can I handle this?' He then walked over to the young would-be thief and put his arm around his shoulder, looked him in the eye for a moment, and said, 'Son, tell me, why are you doing this? Why were you trying to steal that transmission?' Then Mr. Crowley started walking toward the office with his arm around the boy, asking questions about the young man's car problems as they walked. By the time they had arrived at the office, the father said, 'Well, I think your clutch is gone and that's causing your problem.'

"In the meantime, Vern was fuming. 'Who cares about his clutch?' he thought. 'Let's call the police and get this over with.' But his father just kept talking. 'Vern, get him a clutch. Get him a throwout bearing, too. And get him a pressure plate. That should take care of it.' The father handed all of the parts to the young man who had attempted robbery and said, 'Take these. And here's the transmission, too. You don't have to steal, young man. Just ask for it. There's a way out of every problem. People are willing to help.'

"Brother Vern Crowley said he learned an everlasting lesson in love that day. The young man came back to the lot often. Voluntarily, month by month, he paid for all of the parts Vic Crowley had given him, including the transmission. During those visits, he asked Vern why his dad was the way he was and why he did what he did. Vern told him something of their Latter-day Saint beliefs and how much his father loved the Lord and loved people. Eventually the would-be thief was baptized. Vern later said, 'It's hard now to describe the feelings I had and what I went through in that experience. I, too, was young. I had caught my crook. I was going to extract the utmost penalty. But my father taught me a different way.'"[3]

The Savior said, "I, the Lord, will forgive whom I will forgive, but of you it is required to forgive all men," and "if ye forgive men their trespasses your heavenly Father will also forgive you" (D&C 64:10; 3 Nephi 13:14).

CONSECRATION BRINGS CLEANSING

On various occasions and in holy places we are given the opportunity to certify to a loving Father in Heaven that we are willing to dedicate our time, means, and talents to assist in the building of the kingdom. The largesse of countless Saints has been a great blessing in providing needed funds to further the work of the Lord in building chapels and temples, supporting missionary work throughout the earth, expanding the Church Educational System, underwriting the worldwide collection and filming of family history records, providing needed humanitarian assistance in times of disaster to various nations, and blessing countless lives in countries throughout the world.

Saints who truly give their all are senior missionary couples and full-time mission presidents and their wives who interrupt their lives for three years to serve the Lord. A cleansing comes into the lives of these devoted Saints who put all other concerns on hold while they go forward with an eye single to the glory of God.

It was a great blessing for my wife, Dorothea, and me to tour a mission with a devoted mission president and his wife. Without being unduly dramatic, they described their lives and marriage as being rather unfulfilling before being introduced to the gospel twenty years before. As a young couple, they had been addicted to tobacco. The husband confessed that he had an extremely foul mouth and that he included profanity and obscenities in nearly every sentence. They had one young child when they were introduced to the Church, but their main goals in life were financial survival and, if possible, financial success.

The husband spent most waking hours busily engaged in the hectic enterprise of making a living, with the acquisition of material things as his main motive. Then one day a business colleague invited this couple to visit a Sunday meeting at his local church. At first they resisted, but with some good-natured coaxing, they finally agreed to visit church just once. The experience was not entirely unpleasant, but they were not too excited about attending further meetings.

After a period of fits and starts, the young couple agreed to take the missionary discussions, but the match between teachers and students was not a good one. Because the missionaries were teaching the couple in their home, both husband and wife felt it perfectly natural to continue smoking in their own house. When one of the missionaries took exception to their smoking and untactfully asked them to desist, they were offended. Furthermore, whenever the bright and insightful wife asked perceptive questions, the young elders always looked at the husband while giving their answer. The couple ended the missionary discussions after only a few weeks.

Then things happened as they sometimes do under the Lord's watchful eye. The young husband's business colleague put another companionship of missionaries on his trail. During the first meeting with the new elders, the husband said he was not interested in receiving six discussions; rather, he had a long list of questions he wanted answered. But when the couple asked a question, the missionaries would frequently say, "We'll be happy to answer that for you, but first we need to provide a little background to our answer." Unbeknownst to the couple, the missionaries did, in fact, teach them the six missionary discussions, but they did it in such a natural way that the discussions did not appear to be highly structured lessons.

The Word of Wisdom was a great challenge for both the husband and wife, who had forfeited much of their moral agency to tobacco. But again, strange events began happening in their lives. The husband suddenly became very ill, and during the course of his illness he suffered dramatic and worrisome weight loss. By the time he left the hospital, he had lost all desire to smoke. His wife, however, persisted. Then, to her dismay, she developed an acute bronchial condition that forced her to quit smoking. Finally, they were ready to be baptized.

He was working while she stayed home with their infant child. Though he put in long hours, his remuneration as a salesman was often unpredictably sparse. Tithing was often a challenge for them, but they truly had been converted, and they often paid their tithing when the cupboard was almost bare. But sacrifice brings forth the blessings of heaven, and a marvelous business opportunity opened that gave them financial security and the means to provide for six additional children who blessed their home. Then they were called to leave it all behind and to preside over a mission.

It is always inspiring to hear mission presidents and their wives bear testimony of the truths of the gospel and to hear their gratitude for their pioneer forebears who left European shores to travel to Zion. They thank the Lord for all

His bounteous blessings in their lives and in the lives of their children. But the testimonies of this convert couple were different. They focused not on the pioneer trek of their ancestors but on the atonement of Jesus Christ.

With tears streaming down their cheeks, they publicly thanked Him for rescuing them from their sins. Like Alma the Younger, they realized that if they had stayed on their earlier life's course, they would have been denied all the blessings of the restored gospel, the temple, and the privilege of serving a mission. Their leadership is effective among members, missionaries, and investigators because they can testify from first-hand experience of the ecstasy of singing the song of redeeming love after having been snatched from sin.

NOTES

1. Hales, "The Covenant of Baptism: To Be in the Kingdom and of the Kingdom," *Ensign*, November 2000, 6.

2. Faust, "The Refiner's Fire," *Ensign*, May 1979, 59.

3. Hunter, "A More Excellent Way," *Ensign*, May 1992, 62.

NINE

Amulek's Song of the Infinite Atonement

It is expedient that there should be a great and last sac-
rifice; yea, not a sacrifice of man, neither of beast, neither of
any manner of fowl; for it shall not be a human sacrifice;
but it must be an infinite and eternal sacrifice (Alma
34:10).

One of the most compassionate men on our planet is
Harold Thomas, a friend of mine for forty-five years. In
August 1966, Harold and his wife, Margie, went for a summer
stroll after dinner. As they walked along the sidewalk, they
noticed a young girl riding toward them on her bicycle.

To avoid a collision, Brother and Sister Thomas stepped
back to let the girl pass. As they did so, Sister Thomas stepped
off the unusually high curb, lost her balance, and fell backward
into the street.

Her head absorbed most of the impact, and it was quickly
obvious that her injuries were serious. She was rushed to the
hospital for emergency treatment but three days later passed
away, leaving behind her husband and four children. The
family and members of her ward and community felt a great

loss. Those who were especially distraught encouraged Brother Thomas to sue the young girl's family. His response was immediate: There would be no lawsuit and no anger, only forgiveness. Harold said, "That little girl meant no harm, and the money from litigation cannot take away the pain of our loss."

Harold's compassion served his family members well and fortified them for a lesson to be learned later. Twelve years after Sister Thomas' death, Harold's granddaughter was killed in a traffic accident on her way home from college. Brother Thomas went to mourn with and comfort his daughter and her family. The next Sunday he bore his testimony in his daughter's ward and reminded the congregation that his daughter's family was not the only family in sorrow. The driver of the other vehicle, who had fallen asleep while driving and was not injured, was a member of that ward. Her family also felt great sorrow. He importuned ward members to extend their love and forgiveness.

Harold Thomas, having served three times as a bishop and currently serving as a stake patriarch, has claimed the blessings of the infinite atonement throughout his life. He understands well the meaning of the word "infinite" and that the Savior's atoning sacrifice covers more than just the sins of all mankind for the duration of the earth's existence and beyond. The Atonement also eases the pains, afflictions, sicknesses, and infirmities of the children of men (Alma 7:11–15).

LETTING GO

Whenever I enter the sacred precincts of the house of the Lord, I am struck by its beauty, impressed by its feeling of reverence, and delighted to see its workers, who, in their white temple clothing, truly look like angels. One dear sister, though angelic in appearance, never smiled while greeting others. She was reliable regardless of icy roads and inclement weather, and she had a dignified bearing and kindness conducive to reverence in the Lord's house, but she could not or would not smile.

One day a sister temple worker could contain her curiosity no longer. Assuming they had been acquainted long enough to share a few of life's heartaches, the worker asked her sad friend why she never smiled. With tears in her eyes she unfolded her unhappy story. Many years ago she and her husband had taken their children to Yellowstone National Park for a vacation. Because Yellowstone has many geysers, boiling mud pots, and steaming pools, the parents took extra precautions to keep their younger children out of harm's way.

This mother and her three-year-old daughter began walking on the boardwalk near several boiling mud pots. Though the mother held her little girl's hand tightly, in an unguarded moment the youngster squirmed from her mother's grasp, fell off the boardwalk into the mud pots, and quickly sank out of sight. Horrified, the parents looked on helplessly as their precious child disappeared in a split second.

"And since then," the mother said, "I have not been able to smile, nor have I felt like smiling." She paused and added, "That happened over forty years ago, and I just don't think the Lord will ever forgive me for being so careless with one of His little children."

Alma, perhaps as eloquently as any other prophet, has described the infinite, comprehensive nature of the Atonement: "And he will take upon him death, that he may loose the bands of death which bind his people; and he will take upon him their infirmities, that his bowels may be filled with mercy, according to the flesh, that he may know according to the flesh how to succor his people according to their infirmities" (Alma 7:12). As Elder Bruce C. Hafen reminds us, the Atonement is not just for sinners.[1]

The Savior took upon Himself our sins as well as our

mistakes and our heartaches over wayward loved ones. That is why the gospel is called the good news. Because of Christ, it really is okay to smile even though we have made grievous mistakes. Men and women are that they might have joy (2 Nephi 2:25).

INFINITE ATONEMENT

Few missionary companions have been more united than Alma and Amulek. Throughout their labors each testified to and expounded upon that which was taught by the other. Following Alma's profound discussion of the comprehensive, infinite nature of the Atonement, Amulek discussed the qualifications of Christ, who would make the atoning sacrifice. Indeed, Amulek made it clear that only Christ would be able to atone for our sins.

"And now, behold, I will testify unto you of myself that these things are true. Behold, I say unto you, that I do know that Christ shall come among the children of men, to take upon him the transgressions of his people, and that he shall atone for the sins of the world; for the Lord God hath spoken it.

"For it is expedient that an atonement should be made; for according to the great plan of the Eternal God there must be an atonement made, or else all mankind must unavoidably perish; yea, all are hardened; yea, all are fallen and are lost, and must perish except it be through the atonement which it is expedient should be made.

"For it is expedient that there should be a great and last sacrifice; yea, not a sacrifice of man, neither of beast, neither of any manner of fowl; for it shall not be a human sacrifice; but it must be an infinite and eternal sacrifice" (Alma 34:8–10).

For the mother who is unable to smile, Amulek added, "Now there is not any man that can sacrifice his own blood which will atone for the sins of another" (Alma 34:11).

General Authorities occasionally receive letters and phone calls from compassionate parents who plead for help with wayward children. Heartbroken wives write, sometimes with a bit of vindictiveness, criticizing local priesthood leaders who they feel have failed to mete out proper punishment for the sins of their unfaithful husbands. And concerned brothers and sisters ask what can be done to bring prodigal siblings back to the fold.

These heart-tugging concerns are all understandable, and they cause great concern among the Brethren. But one principle remains certain: No human being, as Amulek teaches us, can atone for the sins, mistakes, addictions, and unkindness of another person. No matter how much I love the members of my family, I cannot repent of *their* sins, nor can they take *my* sins upon themselves. Only the Savior can do that, and only upon condition of repentance:

"And he shall come into the world to redeem his people; and he shall take upon him the transgressions of those who believe on his name; and these are they that shall have eternal life, and salvation cometh to none else.

"Therefore the wicked remain as though there had been no redemption made, except it be the loosing of the bands of death; for behold, the day cometh that all shall rise from the dead and stand before God, and be judged according to their works" (Alma 11:40–41).

I fear that pseudo-saviors seek to suffer for others, but their surrogate suffering is in vain. Friends and relatives may become critical of a bishop or stake president who is involved in excommunicating or disfellowshipping their loved one. But none of these relatives would criticize a skilled surgeon for removing a diseased organ, nor would they impede the surgeon in attempting to restore the physical health of his patient.

Nevertheless, some of these same people criticize the performance of spiritual surgery.

President James E. Faust admonished priesthood leaders that those "who have the responsibility of keeping the Church pure must perform this labor in a spirit of love and kindness. It should not be done in a spirit of punishment, but rather of helping. However, it is of no kindness to a brother or sister in transgression for their presiding officers to look the other way."[2]

He then shared some direct counsel by President John Taylor, who said: "I have heard of some Bishops who have been seeking to cover up the iniquities of men; I tell them, in the name of God, they will have to bear . . . that iniquity, and if any of you want to partake of the sins of men, or uphold them, you will have to bear them. Do you hear it, you Bishops and you Presidents? God will require it at your hands. You are not placed in a position to tamper with the principles of righteousness, nor to cover up the infamies and corruptions of men."[3]

Bishops and other leaders must be certain that they do not shoulder burdens that only the Savior can lift. Some burdens of ward members may be shared with others, such as unemployment or underemployment challenges, which may be discussed and resolved in confidence within the ward welfare committee. But many other challenges must be resolved between the person in question and the Savior, and sometimes that requires Church discipline. We refer to Christ as our Savior because He not only saves us from physical and spiritual death but also from lingering guilt, excruciating embarrassment, self-doubt, and despair. In the case of egregious sins, guilt and pain can be removed by the refreshing waters of rebaptism. The Lord's promise is sure: He will consecrate our afflictions for our gain (2 Nephi 2:2).

Pseudo-saviors, in their eagerness to lighten the burdens of sick souls, should share Jacob's concern that he not stumble because of his anxiety for others (Jacob 4:18). We should "mourn with those that mourn" and "comfort those that stand in need of comfort" (Mosiah 18:9), but our faith, prayers, fasting, and continual compassion will reap a more fruitful harvest than our anxiety, fear, criticism, and judging of the judges. The angel who appeared to Alma the Younger did so in response to Alma the Elder's faith and prayers, not because of his father's suffering or embarrassment for his son's sins (Mosiah 27:13–15). Great rewards come to those who "stand as witnesses of God at *all times* and in *all things*, and in *all places*" (Mosiah 18.9, emphasis added).

CHANGING ME

Several years ago Dorothea and I visited one of the European temples in the spring. The temple grounds were awash in the glow of golden tulips that sunny afternoon. Seated on a bench was a lovely sister whose silver hair glistened in the sun. She greeted us so pleasantly that I asked her the reason for her obvious happiness and radiant countenance.

"Well," she replied, "I haven't always been this happy. To tell you the truth, when I was a young woman, I was so eager to get married, I hurriedly married the wrong man. I was very active in the Church, but he did not want to have anything to do with religion."

For many years, her home was filled with strife and contention over her activity in the Church. Her husband seldom attended Church meetings with her and the children, he refused to pay tithing, and he insisted on drinking coffee and beer at home.

"One day I reached the breaking point," she said. "I just felt like I could not take any more of this, so I knelt down and asked Heavenly Father for permission to get a divorce. I wasn't prepared for the answer to my prayer. The Lord clearly told me that if I would change, my husband would eventually change. So I stopped nagging him about his spotty Church attendance and his coffee and beer. I tried to be cheerful and to commend him for the good things he did. I kept going to Church and continued to fast and pray that the Lord would soften his heart."

One Sunday, to her great surprise, her husband decided to accompany her to Church. Soon afterward he was attending Church each Sunday. He quit drinking beer and eventually suggested that the family begin paying tithing. Finally, he quit drinking coffee.

"We began preparing to go to the temple, and that made a great difference in our marriage. Several months ago we were called to be temple ordinance workers, so now we work a couple of days a week. Our marriage still isn't perfect, but we are so grateful for the gospel and for each other that I guess it just shows in our faces."

We can do a lot of things to influence other people's lives, but we cannot suffer for their sins. Nor can we repent for their sins. We may have to suffer because of their sins, but we cannot suffer for and in behalf of them. However, we can pray for them, extend a lifting hand, speak an encouraging word, fast, place their names on prayer rolls in holy places, and trust in the Lord.

FORGIVING THE FOE

War between nations inevitably causes massive physical death and destruction. In addition, it creates a lingering animosity between combatants that, in all too many cases, cankers the souls on both sides long after the conflict has ended. The relationship between Trevor Dakin and Nagase Takashi is a wonderful exception.

Trevor was a young British infantry corporal stationed in Thailand during World War II. Like many of his comrades-in-arms, he was captured in the jungle by the Japanese army and forced to build bridges across the valleys and jungles amidst the Burmese mountains. The prisoners' efforts were immortalized by the movie *The Bridge on the River Kwai*, but that bridge was merely one of 688 bridges built to support a 257-mile railway line. The Japanese predicted that the project would take five years, but thanks to the toil of thousands of prisoners of war and forced Asian laborers, the railway and bridges were completed in only seventeen months. Those forced to work on the project received minimal food rations. An estimated sixteen thousand prisoners of war and approximately ninety thousand Asian laborers were literally worked to death by their Japanese captors.

Nagase Takashi's role in this nefarious scheme was that of interpreter for the brutal interrogators who subjected prisoners to the "third degree"—extracting answers to their questions through intimidation and torture. Nagase returned home after the war, haunted for nearly two decades by memories of his participation in these cruel sessions. Though he never tortured or beat prisoners, he finally gained a measure of relief when he returned to Thailand and laid a wreath in the British cemetery in Kanchanaburi. Prior to this visit he had been in failing health, but, he said, "As I placed the wreath, a pure sound came into my ears and a light poured out from my chest. My health recovered and every time I come here my health gets better."

Nagase Takashi has made more than ninety subsequent visits to Kanchanaburi from his home in Osaka, Japan, and has "financed the studies in Japan of 23 Thai students from the area, built a temple and founded [a] mobile health clinic for remote villages." He has raised more than $800,000 from

remorseful Japanese who have supported his efforts at reconciliation with Thais whose relatives died in the war. He has also
brought together numerous British captives and Japanese captors in a further act of reconciliation. One of these former
British POWs is Trevor Dakin, who has become a true friend
to Nagase Takashi.

"Mr. Nagase is an honorable man who realized the horrible
atrocities committed by the Japanese," Trevor observed. "He
has helped me lay a ghost to rest." The relationship between
Trevor and Nagase is characterized by complete forgiveness,
mutual respect, and reconciliation.[4]

Praise be to Nagase Takashi for his countless good works
in the aftermath of World War II. His efforts at reconciliation
are praiseworthy, but even his best efforts fall short of the One
whose infinite atoning sacrifice can heal all wounds, remove all
scars, and wipe away all tears from all faces regardless of the
cause of those tears.

SYMBOLS OF ATONEMENT

Twenty years ago, Dorothea and I experienced the blessing
of accompanying several Brigham Young University students to
the Holy Land. This was before the construction of the beautiful Center for Near Eastern Studies in Jerusalem, so we found
hospitable lodging in various Israeli Kibbutzim. In one
Kibbutz, as the first three stars appeared in the Friday evening
sky, we were graciously invited to participate in the rites and
rituals associated with the Jewish Sabbath. Two dozen of us
were seated at four long tables arranged in a large rectangle.

I had the good fortune of being seated next to a rabbi.
Another rabbi stood at the head of the rectangular tables and
led our ritual. While singing one of the Psalms in the beautiful
mode of the synagogue cantor, he began breaking two loaves
of bread into smaller pieces. I leaned over to the rabbi next to

me and asked the meaning of the ritual. He replied, "The two loaves represent the two portions of manna the children of Israel gathered on the eve of the Sabbath as they wandered in the desert for forty years."

The broken bread was passed to each person seated around the large tables. The chief rabbi then held up a bottle of grape juice, explaining that juice was being used on this occasion instead of red wine in deference to the Latter-day Saint students present. Again he sang a beautiful, plaintive song, and again I asked my neighbor the meaning of the ritual. He said, "The red wine represents the lamb's blood the children of Israel smeared on their doorposts so the destroying angel would pass over their firstborn children."

Nearing the conclusion of His earthly ministry, the Savior met with His disciples in an upper room to engage in a ritual they thought would be familiar to them. But instead of breaking bread that represented manna in the wilderness, He said to them, "Take, eat; this is my body." He then took the chalice of wine and said, "Drink ye all of it; for this is my blood of the new testament, which is shed for many for the remission of sins" (Matthew 26:26–28).

For those who had eyes to see and ears to hear, it was clear that the law of Moses and the rituals they had practiced for years pointed to the atoning sacrifice of Jesus Christ. The sacrifice of the unblemished lamb at the altar was intended to prepare their minds to receive the sacrifice of the Lamb of God. But most of the Jews in Jerusalem failed to recognize Jesus as the Messiah who fulfilled the law of Moses. Likewise, King Noah's priests, with one exception, failed to make the connection between the preparatory law and the grand event it typified (3 Nephi 15).

Elizabeth Barrett Browning eloquently described this failure to see what needs to be seen:

Earth's crammed with heaven,
And every common bush afire with God;
But only he who sees, takes off his shoes—
The rest sit round it and pluck blackberries.[5]

After Alma gave his great discourse on faith to the multitude upon the hill Onidah, Amulek began to teach them of the infinite atonement. Knowing that the people observed the law of Moses, he explained to them the purpose of the law, "every whit pointing to that great and last sacrifice; and that great and last sacrifice will be the Son of God, yea, infinite and eternal. And thus he shall bring salvation to all those who shall believe on his name; this being the intent of this last sacrifice, to bring about the bowels of mercy, which overpowereth justice, and bringeth about means unto men that they may have faith unto repentance.

"And thus mercy can satisfy the demands of justice, and encircles them in the arms of safety, while he that exercises no faith unto repentance is exposed to the whole law of the demands of justice; therefore only unto him that has faith unto repentance is brought about the great and eternal plan of redemption" (Alma 34:14–16).

NOTES

1. Hafen, *The Broken Heart,* 1–23.

2. Faust, "Keeping Covenants and Honoring the Priesthood," *Ensign,* November 1993, 37.

3. Taylor, Conference Report, April 1880, 78.

4. Thomas Crampton, "A Japanese Atonement Helps to Heal Wounds," *International Herald Tribune,* 10 October 1997, 2.

5. Browning, *Aurora Leigh,* 286.

TEN

Aaron's Song of Sacrificing Sins

And since man had fallen he could not merit anything of himself; but the sufferings and death of Christ atone for their sins, through faith and repentance, and so forth; and that he breaketh the bands of death, . . .

. . . When Aaron had said these words, the king did bow down before the Lord . . . and cried mightily, saying: . . . I will give away all my sins to know thee (Alma 22:14, 17, 18).

The entire Book of Mormon is a counterpoint in contrasting voices of righteousness and evil. King Lamoni (following his conversion) and his father (before his conversion) illustrate one such counterpoint. Shortly after Lamoni's conversion, Ammon learned that his brethren had been cast into prison in the land of Middoni. Inasmuch as Lamoni knew Antiomno, the king of that land, he offered to intercede in behalf of Ammon's brethren. As Lamoni and Ammon made their way to Middoni, they fortuitously met Lamoni's father, whose disposition to do evil was readily apparent in what he said and did. He first castigated his son for not having attended a recent feast given in honor of his sons, and then he condemned his son for associating with a Nephite, "one of the children of a liar" (Alma 20:10).

Trusting that his father would accept his explanation for not having attended the feast, Lamoni was astonished when his father commanded him to slay Ammon. When Lamoni refused, his father tried to slay his own son. But for Ammon's physical intervention, he likely would have done so. In his anger, the king turned his sword on Ammon, but "Ammon withstood his blows, and also smote his arm that he could not use it." Ammon then raised his sword and threatened to smite the king if he did not release his brethren from prison. Fearing for his life, the king offered to grant whatsoever Ammon asked, "even to half of the kingdom" (Alma 20:20, 23).

When the king "saw that Ammon had no desire to destroy him, and when he also saw the great love he had for his son Lamoni," he was astonished. He not only acceded to releasing Ammon's brethren from prison but also assured his son that he could retain his kingdom from then on without paternal governance. Ammon and Lamoni then continued their journey to the land of Middoni, where they secured the release of Ammon's brethren from prison (Alma 20:26–30). Afterward, Ammon and Lamoni proceeded to the land of Ishmael, where Ammon continued teaching Lamoni's people (Alma 21:18–23).

After their release from prison in Middoni, Aaron and his brothers, in best missionary tradition, departed from Ammon and Lamoni with a golden referral to teach Lamoni's father. Lamoni's father was at first somewhat apprehensive and wanted to know why Ammon had not come in person to teach him. Aaron patiently explained that Ammon had been transferred: "The Spirit of the Lord has called him another way" (Alma 22:4). The Spirit had also been working on the unrighteous father of Lamoni, prompting him to ask Aaron, "What is this that Ammon said—If ye will repent ye shall be saved, and if ye will not repent, ye shall be cast off at the last day?" (Alma 22:6).

Aaron systematically sought to ascertain what the king's basic religious beliefs were, including his conception of God. After discerning some embers of belief that could be fanned into faith, Aaron began teaching the king in much the same way Ammon had taught Lamoni. He began with the creation of the world and of Adam, and he discussed the Fall and "the plan of redemption, which was prepared from the foundation of the world, through Christ, for all whosoever would believe on his name" (Alma 22:13).

Aaron taught with unmistakable clarity that "since man had fallen he could not merit anything of himself; but the sufferings and death of Christ atone for their sins, through faith and repentance, and so forth; and that he breaketh the bands of death, that the grave shall have no victory, and that the sting of death should be swallowed up in the hopes of glory" (Alma 22:14). The king subsequently asked what he must do to be born of God, and have "this wicked spirit rooted out of my breast, and receive his Spirit, that I may be filled with joy, that I may not be cast off at the last day?" (Alma 22:15).

Aaron taught the king how to pray, how to call upon the name of the Lord in faith, and how to undergo the pruning process of repentance. In response to Aaron's instructions, this once arrogant, mean-spirited man prostrated himself on the ground in the depths of humility. He then cried mightily, "O God, Aaron hath told me that there is a God; and if there is a God, and if thou art God, wilt thou make thyself known unto me, and *I will give away all my sins to know thee,* and that I may be raised from the dead, and be saved at the last day" (Alma 22:18; emphasis added).

This portion of the king's prayer is one of the most important passages in all holy writ, exemplifying what is required of each of us if we are to some day regain the presence of the Father and the Son. Aaron had taught the king the plan of redemption; with help from the Spirit, the king had understood perfectly. The words of his prayer came from the principles Aaron had taught him by the prompting of the Spirit. Aaron's song had become the king's song of redeeming love.

Although the people at the time of Aaron still observed the law of Moses, Aaron knew that the purpose of animal sacrifice was to point their lives toward Christ's atoning sacrifice. This is what he taught the king. Elder Neal A. Maxwell eloquently reiterated this point: "Real, personal sacrifice never was placing an animal on the altar. Instead, it is a willingness to put the animal in us upon the altar and letting it be consumed!"[1]

Upon recovering from the dramatic physical aftermath of his conversion, the king sent forth a proclamation protecting Aaron and his brethren from any physical harm and persecution during their missionary labors in the land. As a result of the king's aegis, the zeal of the missionaries, and the companionship of the Spirit, "thousands were brought to believe," and "as many of the Lamanites as believed in their preaching, and were converted unto the Lord, never did fall away" (Alma 23:1–6).

A CATHOLIC PRIEST'S CONVERSION

Nearly every convert to the Church is required to give away some old habits and a few friends. Some even have to give up their work. One of the greatest challenges comes to those converts who were once clergy in other churches. While studying at the University of Pittsburgh in the mid-1960s, I met John Staley, who would have a great influence on my life. He was a middle-aged man who had recently been converted to the Church, and he was at the university on a postdoctoral fellowship. He had been on the faculty of St. Vincent's College, a small Catholic college in Latrobe, Pennsylvania, and for twenty-five years he had been a Benedictine monk in the Catholic Church.

He and several other priests had become concerned about the diminution of fellowship and sense of community within their church, and he obtained permission from his superiors to explore this phenomenon at the Institutes for the Achievement of Human Potential in Philadelphia. There he met a graduate student named Mariellen, who just happened to be a Latter-day Saint. He and Mariellen had a number of in-depth discussions about religion, and one day Father John gave her a copy of *The Divine Milieu,* by the French Jesuit priest and paleontologist Pierre Teilhard de Chardin. She felt that many of Teilhard de Chardin's insights were compatible with Latter-day Saint theology, and eventually she developed the courage to invite John to church, where he could observe the vast voluntary participation in the worship services.

Father John arrived at the chapel with notepad in hand. He counted two greeters at the outside door and two more near the chapel. One man conducted the meeting, and one woman played the organ while a second woman conducted the singing. Another man offered the invocation. Two young priests administered the sacrament, and eight young deacons distributed it to the congregation. Two other members gave brief talks following the sacrament.

The man conducting the meeting then indicated that it was time to dismiss for Sunday School class. John discovered that there were teachers and classes for five age groups from twelve through adulthood. He also discovered that there was a junior Sunday School involving yet another organist and chorister and six more teachers for children under twelve. For a period of two hours in that building that morning, at least thirty-three individuals had specific assignments and responsibilities. Father John was impressed!

One of John's favorite authors was Teilhard de Chardin, who, as a paleontologist, had traveled widely, examining the fossil remains of extinct species. He found Darwin's theory of evolution to be a useful taxonomical scheme for classifying animals from very simple to very complex, culminating in the creation of mankind. But Teilhard de Chardin's writings on evolution made biologists and Catholic theologians uncomfortable. The Catholic Church prohibited the publication of his manuscripts during his lifetime. They were published posthumously in 1955.

Teilhard de Chardin believed that the creation of man occurred in a completely different realm than other living beings because of man's freedom of choice, memory, and power of introspection: "Man not only knows; he knows that he knows."[2] He proposed that mankind is involved in a much higher level of evolution, not just at the organic, biological level, but also at the spiritual level. Other biological scientists and geologists were concerned primarily with the "*without* of things," such as comparative musculoskeletal, cardiovascular, and neurological development of organisms. But Teilhard de Chardin was concerned with the "*within* of things," the purposeful, spiritual evolution of men and women.[3]

His conclusions concerning organic evolution, in many regards, paralleled those of President Gordon B. Hinckley, who said: "When I was a college student there were many discussions on the question of organic evolution. I took classes in geology and biology and heard the whole story of Darwinism as it was then taught. I wondered about it. I thought much about it. But I did not let it sway me, for I read what the scriptures said about our origins and our relationship to God. Since then I have become acquainted with what to me is a far more important and wonderful kind of evolution. It is the evolution of men and women as the sons and daughters of God, and of our marvelous potential for growth as children of our Creator."[4]

Teilhard de Chardin explored in detail the impact of instincts in the animal kingdom and posed a profound question: "According to current thought, an animal develops its carnivorous instincts *because* its molars become cutting and its claws sharp. Should we not turn the proposition around? In other words if the tiger elongates its fangs and sharpens its claws is it not rather because, following its line of descent, it receives, develops, and hands on the 'soul of a carnivore'?"[5]

He continued this line of reasoning: "In the behavior of a cat, a dog, a dolphin, there is such suppleness, such unexpectedness, such exuberance of life and curiosity! Instinct is no longer narrowly canalised, as in the spider or the bee, paralyzed to a single function. Individually and socially it remains flexible."[6]

After engendering criticism among biological scientists and geologists, Teilhard de Chardin forged ahead in predicting the great power of love in the lives of the earth's inhabitants: "*The day will come when, after harnessing [space], the winds, the tides, [and] gravitation, we shall harness for God the energies of love. And, on that day, for the second time in the history of the world, man will have discovered fire.*"[7]

On occasion I have glimpsed this power of love of which Teilhard de Chardin wrote. I have seen children who have been called stupid by their parents and siblings blossom under the tutelage of a loving teacher. I have seen the love of a senior missionary couple rekindle the embers of testimony in the hearts of less-active members. I have seen the love of a long-suffering mission president transform a scared little boy into a confident young man. I have observed how the sheer power of love can combat chronic bouts of depression, chase away the clouds of self-doubt, and let in the sunshine. This same kind of love has miraculously driven hatred from hurt hearts and regenerated romance in dying marriages. The love of missionaries and members has led countless converts to the source of all truth, and the love of home teachers, bishops, and ward council members has led many members to claim the blessings of the temple.

Teilhard de Chardin was concerned for those living in an existential vacuum in which their lives had little purpose, direction, or meaning. Of these people he wrote, "For the man who sees nothing at the end of the world, nothing higher than himself, daily life can only be filled with pettiness and boredom. So much fruitless effort, so many wasted moments."[8] However, when individuals begin to grasp the idea that there is a purpose to their lives on earth, "the world glows with a new warmth: that is to say, it opens wholly to the power of Love."[9] He added, "It is impossible to love Christ without loving others. . . . And it is impossible to love others . . . without moving nearer to Christ."[10]

As Teilhard de Chardin matured, his writings became less analytical and more prescriptive. For example, he wrote, "If your work is dull or exhausting, take refuge in the inexhaustible and becalming interest of progressing in the divine life. . . . Man can escape the terrible boredom of monotonous and commonplace duty only by facing the inner tension and the anxieties of 'creation.' . . . Over and over again he must transcend himself, tear himself away from himself, leaving behind him his most cherished beginnings."[11]

In the Savior's allegory of the vineyard, He taught, "I am the true vine, and my Father is the husbandman. Every branch in me that beareth not fruit he taketh away; and every branch that beareth fruit, he purgeth it, that it may bring forth more fruit" (John 15:1–2). Teilhard de Chardin's later writings reflected this same pruning principle as he observed that "complete Christian endeavor consists in . . . cherishing the 'hollownesses' as well as the 'fullnesses' of life."[12] This was also the insight gained by King Lamoni's father. In order to receive the fulness of the gospel in his life, he needed to sacrifice all his sins and come to the Lord hollow.

Against the background of Teilhard de Chardin's philosophical writings, one of Father John Staley's discussions with Mariellen led her to say, "As man now is, God once was: as God now is, man may be."[13] When John heard this profound thought, he was astonished and asked her to repeat it. She explained that Lorenzo Snow, a prophet and the fifth president of the Church, had taught this doctrine, coining the couplet from the teachings of the Prophet Joseph Smith. John could hardly contain his excitement. In the ensuing weeks he observed the linkage between Latter-day Saint theology and the organizational structure of the Church. If we are, indeed, to become like God, we must learn to accept incremental responsibilities far and above just showing up for Church on Christmas and Easter Sunday to hear one other person conduct the meeting, deliver the sermon, and dispense communion.

John finally agreed to receive the missionary discussions. The mission president was sorely tempted to teach John himself; however, he felt prompted to send a couple of young, humble, garden-variety elders instead. Father John was impressed and amazed at the ability of these young men to teach the restored gospel in a very systematic and understandable way. The concept of the apostasy and restoration of priesthood authority discomforted the Benedictine monk, but he maintained an open mind and an open heart. John asked several difficult questions, and when the missionaries were uncertain of the answer, they humbly replied, "We don't know, but we will have an answer for you the next time we meet."

Eventually, John decided not only to be baptized but also to marry Mariellen.

The most prominent building on the University of Pittsburgh campus is the 42-story gothic Cathedral of Learning. John had been spending much of his time in Philadelphia and came to Pittsburgh only sporadically, so I was surprised and delighted to meet him one day on the crowded elevator of the Cathedral of Learning. With students and faculty getting on and off at nearly every floor, it is possible to carry on a rather lengthy conversation before reaching one's destination on the upper floors.

I threaded my way over to John's side of the elevator and whispered, "What are you doing in the Church these days in Philadelphia?" Despite two dozen ears in close proximity, John bellowed in his deep, robust voice, "I was ordained an elder in the Melchizedek Priesthood, and now Mariellen and I are participating in the temple preparation seminar. Last week we discussed tithing and the Word of Wisdom." With no small embarrassment, I looked at the startled faces of the other elevator passengers. From John's booming voice, each of them had heard "Melchizedek Priesthood," "temple preparation," and "Word of Wisdom" and had no clue what he was talking about.

A similar experience occurred each time we had lunch together with a few colleagues at the university. Not only those seated at our table had an opportunity to listen to his enthusiastic recounting of his conversion, but so did those seated at neighboring tables. John Staley was not ashamed of the restored gospel of Jesus Christ.

In 1969, when officials at Brigham Young University recruited me to join the faculty, I suggested that they also interview my friend, John, who, since his conversion, referred to himself as "a defunct monk." We joined the faculty at the same time and spent a dozen wonderful years together as colleagues at the university. Then John passed away of a sudden heart attack.

He was a bright yet humble man who, like Lamoni's father, submissively sacrificed to the Lord his previous beliefs and past traditions in order to provide room for the fulness: being baptized by those holding proper authority, receiving the laying on of hands for the gift of the Holy Ghost, being ordained to the Melchizedek Priesthood, receiving the temple endowment, and being sealed to Mariellen for time and all eternity.

John realized that without the merits of Christ's atonement, we, of ourselves, are incapable of regaining the presence of God. John became convinced that "it is by grace that we are saved, *after* all we can do" (2 Nephi 25:23; emphasis added.) For John, the fulness included access to additional scripture and modern revelation that fed his hungry soul. In his emptiness, he found the fulness of the gospel.

NOTES

1. Maxwell, "Deny Yourselves of All Ungodliness," *Ensign*, May 1995, 68.

2. Teilhard de Chardin, *Future of Man*, 138.

3. Teilhard de Chardin, *Phenomenon of Man*, 55, 56, 232.

4. Hinckley, *Faith—The Essence of True Religion*, 18.

5. *Phenomenon of Man*, 150.

6. *Phenomenon of Man*, 156.

7. Teilhard de Chardin, *Toward the Future*, 86–87; emphasis added.

8. *Toward the Future*, 94.

9. *Toward the Future*, 5.

10. Teilhard de Chardin, *Divine Milieu*, 125.

11. *Divine Milieu*, 35, 41.

12. *Divine Milieu*, 67.

13. Snow, *Biography and Family Record of Lorenzo Snow*, 46.

ELEVEN

Ammon's Song of Encircling Love

Behold, how many thousands of our brethren has he loosed from the pains of hell; and they are brought to sing redeeming love. . . . Yea, they were encircled about with everlasting darkness and destruction; but behold, he has brought them into his everlasting light, yea, into everlasting salvation; and they are encircled about with the matchless bounty of his love (Alma 26:13, 15).

In the Doctrine and Covenants we learn that many honest men and women throughout the earth "are only kept from the truth because they know not where to find it" (D&C 123:12). One such seeker of truth was the Danish author and philosopher Søren Kierkegaard.

Kierkegaard was born in Copenhagen in 1813 and died forty-two years later in the same city in 1855, just five years after Erastus Snow introduced the restored gospel to Denmark and only four years after Elder Snow and Elder Peter Hansen translated the Book of Mormon into Danish. It appears that Kierkegaard died unaware of The Church of Jesus Christ of Latter-day Saints in Copenhagen—at least he made no reference to the Church in his writings. Kierkegaard was a philosopher spiritually akin to the courageous reformers of an earlier era who lived at the very edge of the light they had been given and who attempted to correct doctrinal errors in the churches of their day.

Like the reformers, Kierkegaard criticized certain practices of the churches of his day, but he was equally critical of speculative philosophers who viewed Christianity solely as a historical phenomenon. Kierkegaard claimed, "If the speculative philosopher is at the same time a believer . . . he must long ago have perceived that philosophy can never acquire the same significance for him as faith [because] . . . he cannot attach his eternal happiness to speculative philosophy."[1]

I am aware of the caveats of mixing worldly philosophy with holy scripture. My reasons for including excerpts from the thoughts and writings of Teilhard de Chardin in the previous chapter and of Kierkegaard in this chapter are twofold. First, I want to demonstrate that not all philosophers seek to destroy faith by the power of reason. In fact, many philosophers and poets provide us with helpful insights. Second, I want to illustrate that the sure knowledge received by divine revelation through living prophets is far superior to the inspiration of philosophers and poets.

The Apostle Paul described well our days—days in which people are "ever learning, and never able to come to the knowledge of the truth" (2 Timothy 3:7). Teilhard de Chardin, Kierkegaard, and many other great thinkers, both ancient and modern, have sincerely sought for truth, but as Kierkegaard intimated, unless true religion is introduced through apostolic power and authority, it remains a system of ethics devoid of the power to change people's lives.[2] Or, as Paul put it, "*If in this life only* we have hope in Christ [in other words, if Christ was only a great teacher and not the Redeemer and resurrected Son of

God], we are of all men most miserable" (1 Corinthians 15:19; emphasis added).

Some contend that Kierkegaard's writings are pessimistic and gloomy, as reflected by the titles of two of his books: *Fear and Trembling* and *The Sickness unto Death*. But I find in them great hope and faith. In the first treatise, Kierkegaard wrestled with the Lord's test of Abraham's faith by commanding him to sacrifice his son, Isaac. Kierkegaard reasoned that Abraham demonstrated his willingness to obey that command "for God's sake because God demands this proof of his faith."[3] President Hugh B. Brown explained the Abrahamic test even more succinctly when he said that God knew all He needed to know about Abraham, but "Abraham needed to learn something about Abraham."[4]

Kierkegaard posed the question of Abraham's test: "And yet what did he achieve?" He then answered his own question: "God is the one who demands absolute love," and Abraham remained true to his love. Kierkegaard observed that "anyone who loves God needs no tears, no admiration; he forgets the suffering in the love." He concluded that "Abraham is great because of a purely personal virtue."[5]

Jacob understood the purpose of Abraham's test. He explained that "it was accounted unto Abraham in the wilderness to be obedient unto the commands of God in offering up his son Isaac, which is a similitude of God and his Only Begotten Son" (Jacob 4:5). Abraham not only learned more about himself but also more about the God of the universe who actually did give His Son as a sacrifice for the sins of all mankind. Because of the Lord's unique test of his faith, Abraham acquired a much more profound understanding of the Atonement than can be gained by most mortal men.

In his epilogue, Kierkegaard asserted, "Faith is the highest passion in a person. There perhaps are many in every generation who do not come to faith, but no one goes further."[6] If Kierkegaard had lived long enough to have had access to the *Book of Mormon,* he would have read of the brother of Jared, whose faith *did* go further: "And because of the knowledge of this man he could not be kept from beholding within the veil" (Ether 3:19; Alma 32:34). The First Vision of Joseph Smith in the Sacred Grove is another example of knowledge transcending faith.

In *The Sickness unto Death,* Kierkegaard deals with the perpetual problem of despair, which is for him the sickness unto death. He contends that "to be sick *unto* death is to be unable to die, yet not as if there were hope of life; no, the hopelessness is that there is not even the ultimate hope, death."[7]

Kierkegaard maintained that "an individual in despair despairs over *something.*"[8] One source of despair is "not to be conscious of having a self,"[9] or not being aware of one's true identity, such as the prodigal son who misspent his father's goods. He "wasted his substance with riotous living," experienced despair until "he came to himself," and finally realized who he was and that he must humble himself and return to his father (Luke 15:11–32).

A second cause of despair is "not to will to be oneself,"[10] such as Amulek, who initially willed not to do what he should have done and who resisted becoming what he should become. "I did harden my heart, for I was called many times and I would not hear; therefore I knew concerning these things, yet I would not know" (Alma 10:6).

A third seedbed of despair results from unsuccessfully attempting "to will to be oneself,"[11] like Nephi, who continually fell short of his ideal self and exclaimed, "O wretched man that I am! Yea, my heart sorroweth because of my flesh; my soul grieveth because of mine iniquities" (2 Nephi 4:17). But Nephi also understood the remedy for his despair as he declared in a high-spirited soliloquy, "Awake, my soul! No longer droop in sin. Rejoice, O my heart, and give place no more for the enemy of my soul" (2 Nephi 4:28).

To place mankind's mortal struggle in bold relief, Kierkegaard employs a dialectical model of the opposing forces of sin and faith, similar to Lehi's observation to his son Jacob that "it must needs be, that there is an opposition in all things" (2 Nephi 2:11). Because Kierkegaard did not have access to the Book of Mormon, he engaged in a very detailed argument leading to a final conclusion: "This contrast [sin/faith], however, has been advanced throughout this entire book, which at the outset introduced . . . the formula for the state in which there is no despair at all: in relating itself to itself and in willing to be itself, the self rests transparently in the power that established it. This formula in turn, as has been frequently pointed out, is the definition of faith."[12] And thus he concluded his treatise.

It took Kierkegaard an entire book, with the reasoning power at his disposal, to reach a conclusion similar to the doctrine revealed by Moroni in two verses concerning the cause and cure of despair: "Wherefore, there must be faith; and if there must be faith there must also be hope, and if there must be hope there must also be charity. And except ye have charity ye can in nowise be saved in the kingdom of God; neither can ye be saved in the kingdom of God if ye have not faith; neither can ye if ye have no hope. And if ye have no hope ye must needs be in despair; and despair cometh because of iniquity" (Moroni 10:20–22). The Apostle Paul confirmed to the Romans that "whatsoever is not of faith is sin" (Romans 14:23).

In Ammon's missionary homecoming address, he expressed with such exuberance his gratitude to the Lord for the great success he and his brethren had experienced that he was chided for boasting of his accomplishments. He then reflected upon his wicked past prior to his mission and asked rhetorically: "Who could have supposed that our God would have been so merciful as to have snatched us from our awful, sinful, and polluted state? Behold, we went forth even in wrath, with mighty threatenings to destroy his church. Oh then, why did he not consign us to an awful destruction, yea, why did he not let the sword of his justice fall upon us, and doom us to eternal despair?" (Alma 26:17–19).

Within Kierkegaard's framework, Alma and the sons of Mosiah were not in despair until they became conscious of the disparity between their actions and their real, eternal identity. People without a sense of divine identity may engage in promiscuity, drugs, violent crime, and other forms of immorality, but those who know they are children of God do not engage in those activities. The "greater the degree of consciousness" we gain in an eternal sense, "the more intensive the despair" we feel when we consciously persist in sin.[13] Thus, after exercising faith in the atonement of Jesus Christ, Alma the Younger declared that "there could be nothing so exquisite and so bitter as were my pains" before his repentance, and "on the other hand, there can be nothing so exquisite and sweet as was my joy" after he had experienced a mighty change of heart (Alma 36:21).

In his journal entry for February 7, 1846, Kierkegaard revealed a secret aspiration: "My idea is to give up being an author (which I can only be altogether or not at all) and prepare myself to be a pastor."[14] Young Søren, then only thirty-three years old, never realized his ambition to become a man of the cloth. Instead, he was often an object of suspicion among many clergymen of the day because he criticized their demand of proof for faith and their tendency to intellectualize things of the Spirit.

Kierkegaard declared: "Faith does not need [proof]; aye, it must even regard the proof as its enemy. But when faith begins to feel embarrassed and ashamed, like a young woman . . . who secretly feels ashamed of her lover and must therefore have it established that there is something remarkable about him—when faith thus begins to lose its passion, when faith begins to cease to be faith, then a proof becomes necessary so as to command respect from the side of unbelief."[15]

As he finished his central work, Kierkegaard concluded that "the introduction of Christianity into a country may involve merely an aesthetic relationship, *unless it is by an Apostle* . . . otherwise it holds true that unless the individual is changed and steadily continues to change in himself, his introduction of Christianity is no more a religious act than any ordinary act of conquest."[16] Kierkegaard's conviction of the need for an apostle or prophet to introduce Christianity into a country is well-founded. For, as he contends, if the gospel is not introduced by apostolic authority, it has no power to change people's lives; rather, it becomes merely a system of optional ethics, as opposed to binding covenants and ordinances that are outward manifestations of personal covenants.

Kierkegaard did not know of the Lord's revelation specifically indicating that the Twelve Apostles "shall have power to open the door of my kingdom unto any nation" (D&C 112:21; 107:35; 124:128), but he would have accepted it. He was also unaware of the restoration of priesthood keys by John the Baptist, Peter, James, John, Moses, Elias and Elijah, and of the subsequent building of sacred temples wherein ordinances of eternal significance are performed. Nor could Kierkegaard have known that God, in order to help His spiritual offspring overcome sin and become more like Him, had provided priesthood ordinances that promote the perfecting of the Saints.

In his *Concluding Unscientific Postscript*, Kierkegaard observed, "There is nothing new in Christianity in such a sense that it has not been in the world before, and yet it is all new." His intensive study of the life of Abraham taught him that Abraham's life incorporated the Christian principles taught during Christ's ministry. Then, in an oblique reference to the churches of his day, he asked, "So in case one were to use the name of Christianity and the name of Christ, but the [characteristic beliefs] are anything but Christian, is this then Christianity?"[17] Some of these characteristic beliefs in question would include the extra-biblical Nicene Creed, which reflects a concept of God incongruent with the scriptures, and the practice of infant baptism, also foreign to holy writ.

When the Dead Sea Scrolls were discovered, certain biblical scholars feared that they might indicate the existence of Christ's teachings long before He organized His church in the meridian of time. For Latter-day Saints, with their knowledge of the Book of Mormon and the Pearl of Great Price, neither Kierkegaard's observations about "nothing new in Christianity" nor the Dead Sea Scrolls could undermine their faith. The books of Moses and Abraham in the Pearl of Great Price make clear that Christianity and the great plan of happiness existed before the foundations of the worlds were laid, and that the purpose of our existence was determined long before this earth was inhabited. The Book of Mormon is replete with prophetic utterances about the Savior's ministry and atonement centuries before He came to earth, and believers in Christ were called Christians a century before the Savior called His apostles and organized His church (Alma 46:13).

Church members should not be asking whether The Church of Jesus Christ of Latter-day Saints is a Christian church; rather, they should be asking, "Am I a Christian, and do my actions confirm my professed beliefs? Have I really experienced a mighty change of heart?"

A MIGHTY CHANGE OF HEART

I have a longtime friend whose gentle nature and good humor have endeared him to everyone he meets. But such has not always been the case. Many years ago he started a successful business, but as his success increased so did his stress. Some people reduce stress in their lives by engaging in strenuous physical exercise. Others manage stress through reading, watching athletic contests, painting, playing a musical instrument, listening to inspiring music, or attending the temple. My friend chose a less beneficial means of stress management—he turned to alcohol. As business pressures mounted and stress in his life increased, so did his consumption of alcohol. He eventually became an indentured servant to alcohol and its ever-increasing demands.

One winter afternoon he felt the Spirit prompting him to overcome this addiction, which had weakened his moral agency and freedom to choose. He left his office for several hours and drove a considerable distance to a secluded spot outside the city in which he lived. He parked his car and began to walk into a forest of pine trees bedecked with snow. The snow soon reached his knees, but he continued walking. When the snow became so deep that he could walk no farther, he sank to his knees. There, in that evergreen cathedral, he poured out his soul to the Lord, and as he did so the hollowing began.

He pled with all the energy of his heart for strength to overcome his addiction, which had impoverished his spirit and threatened to destroy his soul. He remained on his knees for a very long time, completely oblivious to the chill in the air. Eventually a sweet, purifying spirit began to distill upon his soul, cleansing him from any desire to drink and fortifying him with a firm resolve to keep the covenants he had made with the Lord many years before.

My friend began attending church meetings, where he was encircled about by loving friends. A spiritually sensitive bishop noticed a change in his countenance, for it was obvious he had undergone more than a small change in his life; he had experienced a mighty change of heart. The bishop soon extended a call to him to work with the young men in the ward. He was a natural, enthusiastic youth leader with a great love for the outdoors. The highlight of any trip was watching him crack several raw eggs and swallow them in succession right out of the shell. To a twelve-year-old deacon, that feat was equivalent to wrestling with alligators.

About a year later this good man was called to be the new bishop. He was beloved of the Saints in his ward because of his warmth, humility, and uncommon empathy for those struggling with sin. When he set apart someone for a new calling, his counselors sometimes became nervous because he would place his hands on the person's head and then wait a minute or two before beginning to speak. Those he set apart truly received a blessing from a servant of the Lord. When called upon to administer to the sick, he would often pause in the middle of the blessing and wait upon the Lord. When the Lord's will had been manifest to him, he would proceed. He was a man of few words and not particularly eloquent of speech, and his musical talents were rather limited, but he knew the song of redeeming love and he sang it often and well.

The bishopric, caring home teachers, and quorum members encircled my friend with love when he was struggling to return to the fold. Upon his return, he could identify with Ammon's exuberance following his mission to the Lamanites:

"Blessed be the name of our God; let us sing to his praise, yea, let us give thanks to his holy name, for he doth work righteousness forever. . . . Behold, how many thousands of our brethren has he loosed from the pains of hell; and *they are brought to sing redeeming love*, and this because of the power of his word which is in us, therefore have we not great reason to rejoice?

"Yea, we have reason to praise him forever, for he is the

Most High God, and has loosed our brethren from the chains of hell. Yea, they were encircled about with everlasting darkness and destruction; but behold, he has brought them into his everlasting light, yea, into everlasting salvation; and they are *encircled about with the matchless bounty of his love*; yea, and we have been instruments in his hands of doing this great and marvelous work.

"Therefore, let us glory, yea, we will glory in the Lord; yea, we will rejoice, for our joy is full; yea, we will praise our God forever. Behold, who can glory too much in the Lord? Yea, who can say too much of his great power, and of his mercy, and of his long-suffering towards the children of men? Behold, I say unto you, I cannot say the smallest part which I feel" (Alma 26:8, 13–16; emphasis added).

"ENVELOPED IN HONEY"

The wife of one of our priesthood leaders in northern Europe was not reared in a Latter-day Saint home, and in her late teens she fell in love with an American serviceman living abroad. He was not a member of the Church either. Shortly after they decided to marry he was transferred to the United States. They moved, married, and eventually had a baby girl. Everyone should have been happy, but the husband began to drink and smoke heavily, filling their house with unkindness and cigarette smoke. Life looked bleak for the next three years.

One day two young elders knocked on her door, and though she was hesitant at first to let them into a home strewn with beer cans, she nevertheless opened the door and bade them enter. They gave her a message of hope, explaining to her our Heavenly Father's plan of happiness. As they concluded, the missionaries invited her to Church the coming Sunday. Sensing some resistance, the elders explained that one of the

Church members in her neighborhood would accompany her. Somewhat relieved at this prospect, she agreed to attend.

During the next few days she told her little three-year-old daughter how exciting it was going to be to go to church on Sunday. When Sunday arrived, both mother and daughter dressed in their finest attire and drove to their neighbor's home on the way to church. Unfortunately, the neighbor did not feel well, but she encouraged the new investigator to go on her own.

As the young mother arrived at the church parking lot with her little girl, fear and anxiety struck her. All the other cars seemed to be filled with intact families: father, mother, and three or four children. She was not certain she belonged there.

In a panic, she turned on the ignition and started to drive away, but her little three-year-old asked, "Where are we going, Mommy?" Her mother replied, "Back home." The little girl protested, "But, Mommy, you promised to take me to church on Sunday." The cherubic daughter's plea melted her heart, so the mother parked the car again and dug deep for the courage to enter the chapel with her little girl.

As they entered, "We were enveloped in a wave of honey!" she later exclaimed. One of the older members picked up her little daughter, hugged her, and asked, "What's your name, little angel?" With outstretched hands, several other members quickly welcomed the anxious mother. They introduced themselves as "brother" and "sister." She immediately felt that she had become part of a family and that she had come home.

President Gordon B. Hinckley considers good friends to be among the key ingredients in retaining new converts, and Robert Browning eloquently described why this is so:

> *Were I elect like you,*
> *I would encircle me with love, and raise*
> *A rampart of my fellows; it should seem*

Impossible for me to fail, so watched
By gentle friends who made my cause their own.[18]

In due time this believing sister parted ways with her unkind husband and returned to her homeland, where she later married a returned missionary in the temple and had her little girl sealed to them. Her new husband is now a local leader of the Church, and they have several children, all of whom are committed to building the kingdom.

ENCIRCLED BY LOVE

One of the most memorable talks I have ever heard was given at a baptism in Vienna, Austria, by Brother Ronald Pope. Brother Pope drew an organizational flowchart of the Church on a chalkboard. At the top was the First Presidency, followed by the Quorum of the Twelve Apostles. Beneath the Twelve were the Seventy and the Area Presidency. Then came the stake presidency and the bishopric. At the bottom, Brother Pope depicted the individual member as a stick figure.

He then discussed how Church members follow the counsel and direction of their file leaders. Then he suddenly turned the chalkboard over. On the opposite side was an inverted organizational flowchart with the name of the newly baptized member on top. Beneath his name were the home teachers, the bishopric, the stake presidency, the Area Presidency, the Quorum of the Twelve, and the First Presidency. Brother Pope concluded by saying, "See how many wonderful people there are in the Church who love you and support you and want you to succeed."

When we returned home from our three-year mission to Austria, the plane arrived at the airport rather late in the evening after a long transatlantic flight. We were eager to reach our house and see our neighbors again, and as we rounded the corner and turned down our street, we were overwhelmed to see on the curb in front of every house a paper sack with a little candle burning inside. The headlights from our car illuminated a yellow ribbon attached to every mailbox on either side of the street. As we reached our driveway, we choked back tears as we beheld our old maple tree completely adorned with yellow ribbons. In the words of Ammon, we were "encircled about with the matchless bounty of his love," which was demonstrated by His children.

NOTES

1. Kierkegaard, *Concluding Unscientific Postscript,* 52–55.
2. *Concluding Unscientific Postscript,* 388.
3. Kierkegaard, *Fear and Trembling,* 59–60.
4. Madsen, *The Highest in Us,* 49.
5. *Fear and Trembling,* 73, 120, 59.
6. *Fear and Trembling,* 122.
7. Kierkegaard, *Sickness Unto Death,* 18.
8. *Sickness Unto Death,* 19.
9. *Sickness Unto Death,* 13.
10. *Sickness Unto Death,* 13.
11. *Sickness Unto Death,* 13.
12. *Sickness Unto Death,* 131.
13. *Sickness Unto Death*, 42.
14. *Concluding Unscientific Postscript*, xiii.
15. *Concluding Unscientific Postscript*, 31.
16. *Concluding Unscientific Postscript*, 388; emphasis added.
17. *Concluding Unscientific Postscript*, 480.
18. Browning, *Poetical Works of Robert Browning*, 1:25.

TWELVE

King Anti-Nephi-Lehi's Song of the Spirit

I thank my great God that he has given us a portion of his Spirit to soften our hearts . . . I also thank my God . . . that he hath forgiven us of those our many sins and murders which we have committed, and taken away the guilt from our hearts, through the merits of his Son (Alma 24:8, 10).

The Savior likened the workings of the Spirit to a gentle breeze whose origins and destinations are indiscernible. Learning to respond to the prompting of the Spirit takes practice (John 3:8). After the massive destruction in ancient America concomitant to the Savior's crucifixion, the voice of Christ pierced the darkness as He instructed the Nephites to no longer offer blood sacrifices and burnt offerings but to bring forth the sacrifices of a broken heart and a contrite spirit. "And whoso cometh unto me with a broken heart and a contrite spirit, him will I baptize with fire and with the Holy Ghost, even as the Lamanites, because of their faith in me at the time of their conversion, were baptized with fire and with the Holy Ghost, *and they knew it not*" (3 Nephi 9:20; emphasis added).

Many of the Lamanites had spent much of their lives in warfare prior to the intercession of Ammon, Aaron, and the Spirit in their lives. Prior to their conversion it would be safe to say that these Lamanites had a dearth of spiritual experiences. Therefore, though they had experienced a genuine conversion and had received baptism and the gift of the Holy Ghost, they were, at least initially, unable to always discern the influence of the Spirit.

The people of Anti-Nephi-Lehi were not the only ones who were slow in recognizing spiritual experiences. A short time after the Savior's first heavenly proclamation to the Nephites, they again heard a voice from the heavens, but "they understood *not* the voice which they heard . . . and . . . again they heard the voice, and they understood it *not* . . . and behold, *the third time they did understand* the voice which they heard" (3 Nephi 11:3, 4, 6; emphasis added). Some of the Nephites had doubted Samuel the Lamanite's prophecies five years previously, and a voice from the heavens was a new and unexpected experience for them. Therefore, it is not surprising that they required God the Father to proclaim His message three times before they finally understood.

RESPONDING TO THE SPIRIT

In His evening encounter with Nicodemus, the Savior explained, "The wind bloweth where it listeth, and thou hearest the sound thereof, but canst not tell whence it cometh, and whither it goeth: so is every one that is born of the Spirit" (John 3:8). The promptings of the Spirit can be ever so subtle, and if we are distracted by other things, the caressing of the gentle breeze to which the Savior alluded may be imperceptible to us.

Regarding the operation of the Spirit in our lives, various Book of Mormon prophets spoke of the "enticings of the Holy Spirit" (Mosiah 3:19), assuring us that the Spirit strives with us

(2 Nephi 26:11–12; Mormon 5:16), contends with us (Alma 34:38), and persuades us to do good (Ether 4:11). The verbs *entice, strive, contend, and persuade* may lie at the gentle end of the continuum of methods of motivation, but they indicate that the Spirit does indeed perform a very active role in our lives if permitted to do so.

The Prophet Joseph Smith observed that "a person may profit by noticing the first intimation of the spirit of revelation; for instance, when you feel pure intelligence flowing into you, it may give you sudden strokes of ideas, so that by noticing it, you may find it fulfilled the same day or soon; (i.e.) those things that were presented unto your minds by the Spirit of God, will come to pass; and thus by learning the Spirit of God and understanding it, you may grow into the principle of revelation, until you become perfect in Christ Jesus."[1]

Elder Dallin H. Oaks has identified "eight different purposes served by communication from God: (1) to testify; (2) to prophesy; (3) to comfort; (4) to uplift; (5) to inform; (6) to restrain; (7) to confirm; and (8) to impel."[2] Perhaps one reason we sometimes fail to act upon the gentle promptings of the Spirit is that we may be prompted to do something we were not prepared to do. Sometimes when we pray for comfort the Spirit impels us to forget ourselves in the service of others. Afterward we feel better about our circumstances and are comforted. On other occasions we ask the Lord to lighten our loads when, all along, He has been strengthening us to bear even greater burdens. We plead for immediate relief, and the Lord teaches us patience, which increases our faith.

As we entreat the Lord to help us find solutions to our problems, it is well to recall His words: "For my thoughts are not your thoughts, neither are your ways my ways, saith the Lord. For as the heavens are higher than the earth, so are my ways higher than your ways, and my thoughts than your thoughts" (Isaiah 55:8–9). Our prayers often take the form of expressing a "wish list" rather than following the Savior's example in the Garden of Gethsemane: "*Nevertheless* not *my* will, but *thine* be done" (Luke 22:42; emphasis added). We are often more inclined to command than to listen and learn.

Naaman. When we approach our supplication to our Father in Heaven in the spirit of "nevertheless," we can avoid the Naaman syndrome. You recall the Syrian captain of old who was prompted to do things he was neither expecting nor prepared to do. As Naaman arrived at the tent of Elisha seeking a blessing for his leprosy, he thought to himself, "He will surely come out to me, and stand, and call on the name of the Lord his God, and strike his hand over the place, and recover the leper" (2 Kings 5:11). Instead, Elisha sent a humble servant to tell this proud military leader to bathe himself seven times in the river Jordan. Had it not been for the intervention of his own servant, Naaman might have returned to Syria still a leper. However, his servant entreated him, "My father, if the prophet had bid thee do some great thing, wouldest thou not have done it? How much rather then, when he saith to thee, Wash, and be clean" (2 Kings 5:13). It seems that more of us today are willing to serve as mission presidents than to share the gospel with our next door neighbor, as a living prophet has admonished us all to do.

Oliver Cowdery. Oliver Cowdery came to the three-room frame house of Joseph and Emma Smith on April 5, 1829. Soon thereafter he began to serve as scribe for Joseph as he translated the Book of Mormon. The Lord provided Oliver with a spiritual manifestation confirming the sacred origin of the gold plates, but it was not long before Oliver began to have doubts about the sacredness of the work in which he was engaged. To bolster his faith, the Lord provided Oliver the following revelation through the Prophet:

"Behold, thou art Oliver, and I have spoken unto thee because of thy desires; therefore treasure up these words in thy heart. Be faithful and diligent in keeping the commandments of God, and I will encircle thee in the arms of my love.

"Behold, I am Jesus Christ, the Son of God. I am the same that came unto mine own, and mine own received me not. I am the light which shineth in darkness, and the darkness comprehendeth it not.

"Verily, verily, I say unto you, if you desire a further witness, cast your mind upon the night that you cried unto me in your heart, that you might know concerning the truth of these things.

"*Did I not speak peace to your mind concerning the matter? What greater witness can you have than from God?*" (D&C 6:20–23; emphasis added).

Oliver Cowdery, like Naaman, was inexperienced in discerning the gifts of the Spirit, and thus the Lord found it necessary to remind him that he had, indeed, already received a witness of the work. As with Elijah the prophet, the witness was not in a strong wind, nor in an earthquake, nor in a fire, but in a still small voice (1 Kings 19:11–12).

Nephi. Nephi was one who readily responded to the promptings of the Spirit, confidently declaring that "the Lord giveth no commandments unto the children of men, save he shall prepare a way for them that they may accomplish the thing which he commandeth them." Despite two disappointing encounters with Laban, who kept the record Nephi and his brethren sought, Nephi was undaunted in keeping the Lord's commandment, being "led by the Spirit, not knowing beforehand the things which I should do." But when the Spirit constrained him to slay Laban, his first reaction was to shrink from this command. "Never at any time have I shed the blood of man," he said (1 Nephi 3:7; 4:6, 10).

However, after he was prompted a second time and then a third time, he yielded to the promptings of the Spirit, which spoke to his soul: "It is better that one man should perish than that a nation should dwindle and perish in unbelief" (1 Nephi 4:13). Notwithstanding Nephi's knowledge of the law of Moses, including the Sixth Commandment, his sensitivity to the Spirit led him to do that which would have been reprehensible had it not been directed of God for a higher, sacred purpose.

The Spirit will probably never ask us to do what Nephi did, yet we may share Nephi's initial resistance to the Spirit from time to time. Like Amulek, we are sometimes inclined to confess, "I knew concerning these things, yet I would not know" (Alma 10:6). To Amulek's credit, after a visit from an angel and his encounter with Alma, he listened to his heart instead of his head and followed the course he knew he must take to gain eternal life.

The return of slow learners and latecomers is always a welcome sight within the kingdom of God, but tragic is the plight of all the Agrippas in our midst who sadly confess, "*Almost* thou persuadest me to be a Christian" (Acts 26:28; emphasis added). These are they who live below their spiritual privileges and who reap the consequences of their failure to respond to the Spirit.

Moses. One of the greatest leaders ever to walk the earth was Moses. It was he who appeared to Joseph Smith and Oliver Cowdery in the Kirtland Temple and restored "the keys of the gathering of Israel from the four parts of the earth, and the leading of the ten tribes from the land of the north" (D&C 110:11). When the Lord first called Moses, however, he had to use a few audio-visual aids to get his attention. After God called to Moses from the burning bush, He informed Moses that He would deliver the children of Israel from Egyptian bondage and that Moses would be His instrument in doing so. Moses responded, "Who am I, that I should go unto Pharaoh, and that I should bring forth the children of Israel out of Egypt?" The Lord reassured him, saying, "Certainly I will be with thee" (Exodus 3:11–12).

But as a shepherd, Moses was more attuned to the bleating of sheep than to the importuning of a Divine Shepherd. He resisted the revelation, protesting that if he were to tell the children of Israel what the Lord had asked him to do, they would not believe him. The Lord then asked Moses to cast his rod upon the ground, and it immediately turned into a serpent. When the Lord commanded him to take the serpent by the tail, it turned into a rod again. Jehovah then asked Moses to put his hand into his bosom, and when he removed it, "his hand was leprous as snow." After placing his hand a second time inside his robe, "it was turned again as his other flesh" when he removed it (Exodus 4:6–7).

The Lord then told Moses that if the rod and the leprous hand did not sufficiently impress the people, he should take some water from the river and pour it upon the land, and it would become blood. Notwithstanding these impressive signs, Moses still protested, "O my Lord, I am not eloquent . . . but I am slow of speech, and of a slow tongue." The Lord then reminded him that He had created Moses' mouth and that He "will be with thy mouth, and teach thee what thou shalt say." Moses had tested the Lord's patience. "And the anger of the Lord was kindled against Moses," and so He commanded that Moses use Aaron as his "spokesman unto the people" (Exodus 4:10–16).

Despite this rather rocky beginning, Moses' confidence, courage, and spiritual sensitivity increased with subsequent visits to the Pharaoh. The serial plagues of frogs, lice, flies, boils, hail and fire, locusts, destruction of Egyptian cattle, and destruction of the firstborn of every Egyptian family reinforced

Moses' faith and faithfulness in following the promptings of the Spirit (Exodus 7–11).

Moses' ability to claim the privileges of the Spirit is manifest in his work as the Lord's instrument in parting the Red Sea, healing the bitter waters of Marah, smiting the rock in Horeb, and faithfully following the pillar of cloud by day and the pillar of fire by night for forty years (Exodus 13–17).

Peter. Because of past experience and tradition, Peter had difficulty teaching the gospel to any group other than the Jews. However, after experiencing an enlightening vision, he declared, "Of a truth I perceive that God is no respecter of persons" (Acts 10:34). He was then prepared to teach the gospel to the Italian centurion Cornelius and his gentile friends and family members (Acts 9–10).

Wilford Woodruff. Perhaps few of our modern prophets have been in harm's way more than President Wilford Woodruff. As a young man he experienced a series of several serious accidents that resulted in two broken legs, two broken arms, two broken ankles, a broken breast bone and three broken ribs. He was also scalded in his early youth, frozen, drowned and resuscitated, and thrown from two waterwheels. President Woodruff attributed many of his accidents to an extraordinary interest the prince of darkness had taken in seeking to destroy his life.

Even before he joined the Church, young Wilford sensed not only the tugs and pulls of the devil but also the sweet enticings of the Spirit. In the spring of 1832 he wrote, "The spirit that was upon me day and night said, 'Go to Rhode Island.'" His brother, Azmon, however, thought they should go to New York to find work, so Wilford was persuaded to accompany his brother. Had they gone to Rhode Island as the Spirit had prompted Wilford to do, they would undoubtedly have met Elders Orson Hyde and Samuel Smith, who were preaching and holding public meetings there. As it turned out, Wilford had to wait another eighteen months before being baptized on December 31, 1833.[3]

Following his baptism, and after receiving the gift of the Holy Ghost and the right to the continual companionship of the Spirit, Wilford Woodruff became a powerful missionary by responding to the enticings of the Spirit. On his second mission to England, he was laboring in the little town of Hanley in the West Midlands when he was prompted to travel southward to the Great Malvern Hills. While there, he met John and Jane Benbow, who were members of the United Brethren, a group of approximately six hundred souls who had broken from the Wesleyan Methodist Church in search of the true church of Jesus Christ. Within a matter of days, Brother Woodruff baptized virtually the entire congregation of United Brethren.[4]

Throughout his apostleship and tenure as president of the Church, Wilford Woodruff seemed always to be in tune with the Spirit whenever extremely difficult decisions had to be made. His humility, meekness, and willingness to be taught qualified him for the privileges of the Spirit.

Enoch. Moses and many modern prophets have not been the only ones to doubt their abilities when called of the Lord. When Jehovah called Enoch, he responded in bewilderment, "Why is it that I have found favor in thy sight, and am but a lad, and all the people hate me; for I am slow of speech; wherefore am I thy servant?" (Moses 6:31). Notwithstanding his initial self-doubts, Enoch learned to listen to the Lord and to persist in doing all that was expected of him, including leading his people in righteousness. His longsuffering and patience paid off when, after 430 years on earth, he was translated along with the city of Zion.

Jeremiah. Of all the prophets in any dispensation of time, few have faced more obstacles or spent more time in dark, damp dungeons than Jeremiah. The fifty-two chapters recording his ministry are punctuated with pathos and pain, and at the conclusion of his record appears a five-chapter post-script titled "The Lamentations of Jeremiah." Though he may have been aware of the doctrine that "men are, that they might have joy" (2 Nephi 2:25), it is not readily reflected in his writings.

During one particular season of rejection and persecution, Jeremiah confessed that "the word of the Lord was made a reproach unto me, and a derision, daily. Then I said, I will not make mention of him, nor speak any more in his name. *But his word was in mine heart as a burning fire shut up in my bones, and I was weary with forbearing, and I could not stay*" (Jeremiah 20:8–9, emphasis added).

The Savior taught His disciples that "the Comforter, which is the Holy Ghost, whom the Father will send in my name, he shall teach you all things, and bring all things to your remembrance, whatsoever I have said unto you" (John 14:26). The Spirit reminded Jeremiah of the word of God he had heard, impelling him to act rather than to shrink from the fray. Often the Spirit sends us toward the sound of guns and hedges up the trail of retreat. In short, the Spirit comforts the afflicted and afflicts the comfortable.

Adam. Because of the fall of Adam, many in modern Christendom condemn Adam and Eve for their transgression. However, Lehi made it abundantly clear to his son Jacob that "if Adam had not transgressed he would not have fallen, but he would have remained in the garden of Eden." Furthermore, Adam and Eve "would have had no children. . . . Adam fell that men might be; and men are, that they might have joy" (2 Nephi 2:22, 23, 25). We revere Adam as the mortal father of mankind and Eve as the mother of all living.

Adam established a reliable pattern of obedience for his posterity. After Adam and Eve had been driven out of the

Garden of Eden and had become mortal, the Lord gave them commandments, one of which was the law of sacrifice. "And after many days an angel of the Lord appeared unto Adam, saying: Why dost thou offer sacrifices unto the Lord? And Adam said unto him: I know not, save the Lord commanded me.

"And then the angel spake, saying: This thing is a similitude of the sacrifice of the Only Begotten of the Father, which is full of grace and truth. . . . And in that day the Holy Ghost fell upon Adam" (Moses 5:6, 7, 9). Adam's obedience is a great lesson for all of us. Even when we do not fully understand all the ramifications of a commandment, we will eventually receive all the blessings predicated upon that commandment if we strive with all our might to comply with it.

Abraham. Abraham, the father of nations and patriarch through whom the Lord made a grand and panoramic covenant, was another servant of God who did not have to be told in great detail what was expected of him. After waiting a full century for the birth of his son, Isaac (Genesis 17:17), Abraham was commanded to go to Mount Moriah and "offer him there for a burnt offering" (Genesis 22:2). Most mortal men might begin to barter with the Lord and try to postpone the execution of the commandment, perhaps even as Abraham sought to delay the destruction of Sodom (Genesis 18:23–33). But on this occasion, "Abraham rose up early in the morning . . . and went unto the place of which God had told him" (Genesis 22:3). *Early,* rather than late or eventually, distinguishes this great patriarch from many of the rest of us.

There is something significantly different in the form and content of home teaching visits during the first few days of the month as compared to visits during the last day of the month. Last-minute visits convey a message over and above the actual message given.

Philip. After the Twelve Apostles called him as one of the seven who would assist them in spreading the gospel, Philip the evangelist, like Abraham, did not need to be told twice what to do. As Philip was laboring in the north part of the country, an angel of the Lord prompted him to go southward through Jerusalem and over to Gaza. There he saw a prominent Ethiopian, a treasurer to Queen Candace, who was seated in his chariot reading Isaiah. The Spirit prompted Philip to introduce himself to the Ethiopian, and "Philip ran thither to him" (Acts 8:30). It is one thing to respond to the Spirit by walking and another to respond by running.

As Philip approached the Ethiopian he asked him if he understood what he was reading from the ancient text, and the Ethiopian replied, "How can I, except some man should guide me?" He invited Philip to climb into his chariot and instruct him. The Ethiopian did not understand to whom Isaiah referred when prophesying, "He was led as a sheep to the slaughter." Philip testified that Isaiah was speaking of Jesus Christ. As they continued traveling together they came to a body of water. The Ethiopian asked Philip, "See, here is water; what doth hinder me to be baptized?" (Acts 8:31–36).

Philip then interviewed him for baptism and asked if he believed in Christ with all his heart. The Ethiopian responded, "I believe that Jesus Christ is the Son of God." After Philip baptized him, the new convert "went on his way rejoicing" (Acts 8:37–39).

Alma the Younger. Notwithstanding Alma's faltering start on the pathway to perfection, once he responded to the angelic ministrations that changed the direction of his life in his youth, he was qualified to receive additional heavenly guidance (Mosiah 27:13–15). After being ejected from Ammoniah, he was "weighed down with sorrow, wading through much tribulation and anguish of soul." An angel then appeared and commanded him to return to the very city in which the people "reviled him, and spit upon him, and caused that he should be cast out of their city" (Alma 8:14, 13).

The evidence was quite convincing that the folks in Ammoniah were not your typical golden investigators. In fact, Alma risked physical harm by returning. Nevertheless, "after Alma had received his message from the angel of the Lord he returned *speedily* to the land of Ammoniah" (Alma 8:18; emphasis added). As Abraham's kindred spirit, Alma did not postpone that which he had been commanded to do merely because it was difficult, unpleasant, and perhaps even life threatening.

Occasionally we may be inclined to implore the Lord to change our circumstances when His solution to our problem impels us to undergo a mighty change of heart. We may seek His confirmation for taking a certain course of action, but instead of confirming our plan, He restrains us with protective promptings that mercifully modify our plans with midcourse corrections. We may aspire to receive a testimony-strengthening theophany in a sacred grove or on a Damascus road, but the Spirit prompts us to search the scriptures, therein finding the source of strength we seek: "These words are not of men nor of man, but of me; for it is my voice which speaketh them unto you; for they are given by my Spirit unto you, and by my power you can read them one to another; . . . wherefore, you can testify that *you have heard my voice,* and know my words" (D&C 18:34–36; emphasis added).

Joseph Smith. Many of the revelations Joseph Smith received were in response to his having prayerfully studied various scriptures and then importuned the Lord to expand his knowledge and understanding. The prophetic mission of Joseph Smith was made possible because a young man, unschooled in the ways of the world, claimed the privileges of the Spirit in a grove of trees, in the Kirtland Temple, in Liberty

Jail, and in countless other places made sacred through the sanctification of the Spirit.

Anti-Nephi-Lehi. The behavior of the Anti-Nephi-Lehies subsequent to their baptism by fire undeniably demonstrated that they had undergone a mighty change of heart. This is evident from the prompting to bury their weapons of war deep in the earth because, as they themselves declared, "It has been all that we could do . . . to repent sufficiently before God that he would take away our stain" (Alma 24:11).

Speaking in behalf of the recently converted citizens of his kingdom, King Anti-Nephi-Lehi sang the following song of redeeming love:

"I thank my God, my beloved people, that our great God has in goodness sent these our brethren, the Nephites, unto us to preach unto us, and to convince us of the traditions of our wicked fathers.

"And behold, I thank my great God that he has given us a portion of his Spirit to soften our hearts, that we have opened a correspondence with these brethren, the Nephites.

"And behold, I also thank my God, that by opening this correspondence we have been convinced of our sins, and of the many murders which we have committed.

"And I also thank my God, yea, my great God, that he hath granted unto us that we might repent of these things, and also that he hath forgiven us of those our many sins and murders which we have committed, and taken away the guilt from our hearts, through the merits of his Son. . . .

"Now, my best beloved brethren, since God hath taken away our stains, and our swords have become bright, then let us stain our swords no more with the blood of our brethren.

"Behold, I say unto you, Nay, let us retain our swords that they be not stained with the blood of our brethren; for perhaps, if we should stain our swords again they can no more be washed bright through the blood of the Son of our great God, which shall be shed for the atonement of our sins.

"And the great God has had mercy on us, and made these things known unto us that we might not perish; yea, and he has made these things known unto us beforehand, because he loveth our souls as well as he loveth our children; therefore, in his mercy he doth visit us by his angels, that the plan of salvation might be made known unto us as well as unto future generations.

"Oh, how merciful is our God! And now behold, since it has been as much as we could do to get our stains taken away from us, and our swords are made bright, let us hide them away that they may be kept bright, as a testimony to our God at the last day, or at the day that we shall be brought to stand before him to be judged, that we have not stained our swords in the blood of our brethren since he imparted his word unto us and has made us clean thereby.

"And now, my brethren, if our brethren seek to destroy us, behold, we will hide away our swords, yea, even we will bury them deep in the earth, that they may be kept bright, as a testimony that we have never used them, at the last day; and if our brethren destroy us, behold, we shall go to our God and shall be saved" (Alma 24:7–10, 12–16).

DEVELOP AN ATTITUDE OF GRATITUDE

The woman who washed the Savior's feet with her tears and dried them with her hair exemplified gratitude commensurate with the sins of which she had been forgiven (Luke 7:37–50). Such was also the case with the Anti-Nephi-Lehies, whose king repeatedly expressed gratitude for his people's second chances. After having received forgiveness of their sins, they faced the prospect of being destroyed by some of their unrepentant brethren. But they were willing to take that risk. A heart filled with gratitude has little room for fear.

The Lord reminds us that "in nothing doth man offend God, or against none is his wrath kindled, save those who confess not his hand in all things, and obey not his commandments" (D&C 59:21). In that light, President Thomas S. Monson has admonished us to develop "an attitude of gratitude," for grateful hearts are susceptible to the prompting of the Spirit.[5]

Alma exhorted the Saints in the valley of Gideon to ask for "whatsoever things ye stand in need, both spiritual and temporal; always returning thanks unto God for whatsoever things ye do receive" (Alma 7:23). It is well to note that Alma did not say "whatsoever *good* things" or "*desirable* things ye do receive." One of the measures of our meekness and true repentance is our inclination to thank a loving Father in Heaven for our trials, tribulations, and disappointments, which, like spiritual push-ups, make us stronger and increase our spiritual stamina so that we might endure to the end.

NOTES

1. Smith, *Teachings,* 151.
2. Oaks, "Revelation," 25.
3. Cowley, *Wilford Woodruff,* 30.
4. Cowley, 116–17.
5. Monson, "An Attitude of Gratitude," *Ensign,* May 1992, 54–60.

THIRTEEN

Helaman's Song of Remembrance

And now, my sons, remember, remember that it is upon the rock of our Redeemer, who is Christ, the Son of God, that ye must build your foundation; that when the devil shall send forth his mighty winds, yea, his shafts in the whirlwind, yea, when all his hail and his mighty storm shall beat upon you, it shall have no power over you to drag you down to the gulf of misery and endless wo, because of the rock upon which ye are built, which is a sure foundation, a foundation whereon if men build they cannot fall (Helaman 5:12).

A s a young British lad, Roger Payne had the good fortune of having a boyhood friend, Alan Teasdale, whose family had recently joined the Church. Members of Roger's family did not attend their own church regularly, so Roger sometimes attended church with Alan. Around age eighteen, Roger took the missionary discussions. Everything the missionaries taught him impressed his young mind for good, and he soon expressed a desire to be baptized.

His father, who loved him and wanted to protect him from the influence of strange religious movements, suggested that he wait a few years before being baptized to make sure that he really wanted to join the Church. If, when he reached twenty, he felt the same way, his father would have no objections. Roger loved his parents and felt duty bound to abide by their counsel. As the months and years passed, his enthusiasm for the Church waned. The Spirit, which Roger had once felt so strongly, apparently withdrew from him.

There is a difference between the influence of the Holy Ghost and the gift of the Holy Ghost. The Prophet Joseph Smith taught that the Holy Ghost, which moved upon Cornelius, would have withdrawn itself had he not responded to its influence and requested that Peter teach him.[1] Upon being baptized, we receive the right to the continual companionship of the Spirit, provided we live worthily.

Roger eventually moved to Chicago for a time, where he occasionally attended church meetings. When he returned to England, he lost all contact with the Church, but whenever he felt impending danger he would remember Alan Teasdale's teenage warning: "Don't die in your sins." The months merged into years and the years into decades. One day, thirty years after his initial encounter with the missionaries, Roger felt a hollowness in his life while reading the Book of Mormon. But he remembered where to go to be filled.

In the summer of 1996 he consulted the Greater Birmingham telephone directory for the phone number of The Church of Jesus Christ of Latter-day Saints in Solihull, a suburb of Birmingham. Brother John Ashmead answered Roger's phone call in the chapel and assured him that missionaries would come to teach him. John and his wife, Irene, met with him and found him to be a golden investigator who remembered many of the gospel principles he had been taught in his youth.

Coincidentally, Dorothea and I moved into the Solihull

Ward shortly after Roger Payne's baptism. We became fast friends over the next four years and my wife and I were privileged to go to the London Temple with Brother Payne when he received his endowment; we also went to the Preston and the Salt Lake Temples together.

A few months following his confirmation, we drove together to the London Temple, where Brother Payne was baptized vicariously for many of his male ancestors. A cousin on his father's side and a cousin on his mother's side had fortuitously been engaged in family history work and graciously gave him copies of their research. Brother Payne's experiences in the temple on behalf of his ancestors strengthened his faith and testimony with each return visit. He found particular joy in being baptized vicariously for his father, who died April 6, 1983. The missionaries who first taught him would no doubt be thrilled to know that the long-forgotten seeds they sowed three decades before had borne gospel fruit.

Remembering can bring great blessings; forgetting can lead to tragic consequences.

A young mother forgot to remind her three young children to buckle up as they drove off in the family van. When the van hit a patch of ice and rolled over three times, all the children were seriously injured.

A sheepherder forgot to light the kerosene lamp on the back of his wagon as he was herding his sheep up a country road after sundown. The driver of a big truck saw them too late and plowed into the herd at full speed. An elderly man forgot his nitroglycerin pills and had an angina attack during a football game. A young married woman forgot her temple covenants when her boss invited her to his bachelor apartment for a candlelight dinner.

In Deuteronomy, Moses admonished the children of Israel to remember who they were "lest [they] forget the covenant of the Lord [their] God." He reminded them to "beware lest thou forget the Lord, which brought thee forth out of the land of Egypt, from the house of bondage." And he urged each of them to "take heed to thyself, and keep thy soul diligently, lest thou forget the things which thine eyes have seen, and lest they depart from thy heart all the days of thy life: but teach them thy sons, and thy sons' sons" (Deuteronomy 4:23; 6:12; 4:9).

It is safe to assume that Helaman had access to the writings of Moses on the plates of brass. To ensure that his two sons never forgot their spiritual heritage, Helaman named them Lehi and Nephi, respectively, reminding them, "I have given unto you the names of our first parents who came out of the land of Jerusalem; and this I have done that when you remember your names ye may remember them; and when ye remember them ye may remember their works; and when ye remember their works ye may know how that it is said, and also written, that they were good" (Helaman 5:6).

Then, as if following Moses' script in detail, Helaman said: "O remember, remember, my sons, the words which king Benjamin spake unto his people; yea, remember that there is no other way nor means whereby man can be saved, only through the atoning blood of Jesus Christ, who shall come; yea, remember that he cometh to redeem the world. . . .

"And he hath power given unto him from the Father to redeem them from their sins because of repentance; therefore he hath sent his angels to declare the tidings of the conditions of repentance, which bringeth unto the power of the Redeemer, unto the salvation of their souls.

"And now, my sons, remember, remember that it is upon the rock of our Redeemer, who is Christ, the Son of God, that ye must build your foundation; that when the devil shall send forth his mighty winds, yea, his shafts in the whirlwind, yea, when all his hail and his mighty storm shall beat upon you, it shall have no power over you to drag you down to the gulf of misery and endless wo, because of the rock upon which ye are built, which is a sure foundation, a foundation whereon if men build they cannot fall" (Helaman 5:9, 11–12).

Young Sister Erika Greiner in Stuttgart, Germany, remembered the rock of her Redeemer, for she had been taught well by righteous parents. But it is often challenging for young women in certain parts of the world to meet worthy young Latter-day Saint men. Sometimes young Latter-day Saint women marry members of other faiths in hopes that they will join the Church some day.

Such was the case with Sister Greiner. The selection of prospective husbands in Germany was sparse when she was young, especially after their ranks had been decimated by World War II. So she married a young man who was tall, dark, and handsome but who did not share her religious beliefs. Herr Metzner raised little objection to her rearing their children in the Church, but for him the Church held little attraction.

Forty years ago, when I was serving as a young missionary in Stuttgart, I visited the Metzner home many times at the south end of streetcar line number fifteen. Time and again we challenged Herr Metzner to be baptized and to prepare to have his family sealed to him in the Swiss Temple. We were especially hopeful during family birthdays or at Christmastime that Herr Metzner would surprise his family with a special gift—the announcement of his impending baptism. But birthdays and three Christmases came and went without the announcement.

Sixteen years after completing my mission, I decided to return to Germany for a visit. It was a great joy to see the German Saints again. I felt as Alma did upon meeting his brethren after a fourteen-year absence. Especially gratifying was the sight of Brother Heinz Metzner seated on the stand in the

chapel at the beginning of Sunday School. He had been baptized and was then serving in the Sunday School presidency.

The bishop asked me to speak in sacrament meeting, and I
felt prompted to speak of the Savior's parable of the sower and
the seeds falling on different kinds of soil. I expressed my joy at
learning of Brother Metzner's baptism, and I discussed the need
of continually nurturing the soil even when the harvest may,
for a time, seem thin. Brother Metzner and I wept tears of
joy, as did his family. His son, Rolf, is currently serving as the
president of the Mannheim Stake in Germany.

NOTE

1. Smith, *Teachings,* 199.

FOURTEEN

Samuel's Song of Signs in the Heavens

And also that ye might know of the coming of Jesus Christ, the Son of God, the Father of heaven and of earth, the Creator of all things from the beginning; and that ye might know of the signs of his coming, to the intent that ye might believe on his name. And if ye believe on his name ye will repent of all your sins, that thereby ye may have a remission of them through his merits (Helaman 14:12–13).

In many of our homes, either on Christmas Eve or Christmas Day, family members gather to sing carols and read the accounts of Matthew and Luke regarding the events surrounding the Savior's sacred birth. Perhaps less frequently we read of that first Christmas from the Nephite perspective half a world away from the manger in Bethlehem.

Five years before the Christ child was born on earth, Samuel, the Lamanite prophet, came among the Nephites to call them to repentance for their ingratitude, pride, and "all manner of iniquities." He testified that they had "sought for happiness in doing iniquity, which thing is contrary to the nature of that righteousness which is in our great and Eternal

Head" (Helaman 13:38). Samuel prophesied that five years hence the Son of God would come to earth to redeem all mankind. As a sign of the Savior's birth, Samuel proclaimed, "There shall be great lights in heaven, insomuch that in the night before he cometh there shall be no darkness . . . as if it were one day and there were no night." The Lamanite prophet also predicted the appearance of a new star and many other wondrous signs in the heavens (Helaman 14:3–6).

He then sang the song of redeeming love: "And if ye believe on his name ye will repent of all your sins, that thereby ye may have a remission of them through his merits" (Helaman 14:13).

But just as Satan sought to prevent Joseph Smith's first uttered prayer, Satan was busily engaged in seeking to destroy the faith of the Nephite nation prior to the Savior's birth. Nephi, the great-great-great-grandson of Alma the Elder, was so concerned about the spiritual welfare of his people that he "cried mightily to his God in behalf of his people, yea, those who were about to be destroyed because of their faith in the tradition of their fathers.

" . . . And behold, the voice of the Lord came unto him saying: Lift up your head and be of good cheer; for behold, the time is at hand, and on this night shall the sign be given, and on the morrow come I into the world, to show unto the world that I will fulfil all that which I have caused to be spoken by the mouth of my holy prophets.

"Behold, I come unto my own, to fulfill all things which I have made known unto the children of men from the foundation of the world, and to do the will, both of the Father and of the Son—of the Father because of me, and of the Son because of my flesh. And behold, the time is at hand, and this night shall the sign be given" (3 Nephi 1:11–14).

President Gordon B. Hinckley has rightly observed, "There would be no Christmas if there had not been Easter. The babe

Jesus of Bethlehem would be but another baby without the redeeming Christ of Calvary, and the triumphant fact of the Resurrection."[1]

Perhaps one reason Christmas carols touch our hearts so deeply is that many of them, like our beloved sacrament hymns, contain the song of redeeming love. For example:

> *Radiant beams from thy holy face,*
> *With the dawn of redeeming grace,*
> *Jesus, Lord, at thy birth.*[2]

> *God rest ye merry gentlemen*
> *Let nothing you dismay,*
> *Remember Christ our Saviour*
> *Was born on Christmas Day;*
> *To save us all from Satan's pow'r*
> *When we were gone astray.*[3]

> *Peace on earth, and mercy mild,*
> *God and sinners reconciled!*[4]

> *Sorrowing, sighing, bleeding, dying*
> *Sealed in the stone-cold tomb.*
> *Glorious now behold Him arise,*
> *King, and God and sacrifice.*[5]

> *And when earthly things are past,*
> *Bring our ransomed souls at last*
> *Where they need no star to guide,*
> *Where no clouds Thy glory hide.*[6]

> *From depths of hell Thy people save,*
> *and give them victory o'er the grave.*[7]

> *And our eyes at last shall see Him*
> *Through His own redeeming love.*[8]

Now ye need not fear the grave:
Peace! Peace! Jesus Christ was born to save.[9]

Good Christian, fear: for sinners here
The silent Word is pleading.[10]

The holly bears a berry,
As red as any blood,
And Mary bore sweet Jesus Christ
To do poor sinners good.[11]

The praises of redeeming love they sang.[12]

Down in a lowly manger the humble Christ was born;
And God sent out salvation that blessed Christmas morn.[13]

Long lay the world, in sin and error pining,
'Till He appear'd and the soul felt its worth.[14]

He comes for our redemption sent.[15]

Yet in thy dark street shineth
The ever lasting Light;
The hopes and fears of all the years
Are met in thee tonight.[16]

These hopes and fears include two great challenges we all face during mortality. The first is the challenge of overcoming sin so that we may become worthy to regain the presence of God. The second is overcoming death. These fears are assuaged by the hope of the healing power of the atonement of Christ. Because of this testimony, we mingle our voices with heavenly choirs at Christmastime in singing, "Glory to God in the highest, peace on earth, good will toward men."

CHRISTMAS TRUCE

Bertie Felstead, who died at the ripe old age of 106 in the summer of 2001, was one of the last surviving participants in the legendary truce between British and German soldiers on Christmas Day in 1914.

World War I had been triggered by the assassination of the Austrian archduke Francis Ferdinand during his visit to Serbia on June 28, 1914. Alliances among nations were mobilized throughout Europe, and after the Germans invaded Belgium on August 3, Great Britain declared war on Germany the following morning.

For the first five months of the war German and British troops dug miles and miles of trenches throughout the fertile French farmland. The trenches provided a degree of protection against mortar and rifle fire. In some cases these trenches were so close that opposing troops could hear the clanging of utensils as enemy soldiers prepared meals.

As Private Bertie Felstead and his compatriot Royal Welch Fusiliers hunkered down in their muddy trench on Christmas Eve, they imagined hearing strains of a familiar Christmas carol floating on the air. As they sharpened their hearing, it became clear that a young German soldier was singing "Stille Nacht, Heilige Nacht," familiar to the British soldiers as "Silent Night."

The Brits rejoined with "God Bless You Merry, Gentlemen," and the Germans followed with "O Tannenbaum."

A British soldier spotted a frail evergreen tree with lighted candles the German soldiers had hoisted atop the sandbags in front of their trench. At the crack of dawn each side beheld hastily fashioned signs that said, "Merry Christmas" or "Frohe Weihnachten."

Then, almost as if on cue, the soldiers from each side laid down their arms. Bertie recalled, "The Germans started it, coming out of their trenches and walking over to us. Nobody decided for us—we just climbed over our parapet and went over to them. We thought nobody would shoot at us if we all

mingled together." What followed would become etched forever in Bertie Felstead's memory.

Someone produced a ball and the men spontaneously
joined in a game of soccer. Soldiers shared photos of loved ones
and swapped holiday greetings and gifts of candy and cigarettes. All too soon, however, the truce was over as officers
ordered the men to return to their respective trenches. But for
a fleeting moment, young soldiers far from home briefly forgot
their allegiance to king and kaiser and paid homage to the
Prince of Peace.[17]

THE GIFT OF FORGIVENESS

When the Savior taught the Nephites how to pray and gave
them the pattern known as the "Lord's Prayer," among other
things He prayed, "And forgive us our debts, as we forgive our
debtors" (3 Nephi 13:11).

After concluding His prayer He reiterated this point: "For, if
ye forgive men their trespasses your heavenly Father will also
forgive you; but if ye forgive not men their trespasses neither
will your Father forgive your trespasses" (3 Nephi 13:14–15).

In Latter-day revelation He underscored the importance of
the miracle of forgiveness:

"Wherefore, I say unto you, that ye ought to forgive one
another; for he that forgiveth not his brother his trespasses
standeth condemned before the Lord; for there remaineth in
him the greater sin. I, the Lord, will forgive whom I will forgive, but of you it is required to forgive all men" (D&C
64:9–10).

I pray that at Christmas and on each day throughout the
year we will give the greatest gift of all, the gift of forgiveness.
May we make those phone calls, write those letters, and pay
those visits needed to make things right throughout the entire
year.

NOTES

1. Hinckley, "The Wondrous and True Story of Christmas," *Ensign,* December 2000, 5.

2. *Hymns,* no. 204.

3. "God Rest Ye Merry Gentlemen," *A Treasury of Christmas Songs,* 10.

4. *Hymns,* no. 209.

5. "We Three Kings of Orient Are," *A Treasury of Christmas Songs,* 188–89.

6. "As with Gladness Men of Old," *Reader's Digest Merry Christmas Songbook,* 183.

7. "O Come, O Come Emmanuel," *A Treasury of Christmas Songs,* 134–35.

8. "Once in Royal David's City," *A Treasury of Christmas Songs,* 187.

9. "Good Christian Men, Rejoice," *Reader's Digest Merry Christmas Songbook,* 178.

10. "What Child Is This?" *A Treasury of Christmas Songs,* 51.

11. "The Holly and the Ivy," *A Treasury of Christmas Songs,* 40.

12. "Christians, Awake, Salute the Happy Morn," *A Treasury of Christmas Songs,* 115.

13. "Go Tell It on the Mountain," *Reader's Digest Merry Christmas Songbook,* 207.

14. "O Holy Night," *A Treasury of Christmas Songs,* 198.

15. "All Hail to Thee," *Reader's Digest Merry Christmas Songbook,* 2000.

16. *Hymns,* no. 208.

17. "Vet of Christmas Truce During WWI Dies at 106," *Deseret News,* 26 July 2001, A12.

FIFTEEN

The Savior's Song of Redeeming Love

Behold I have given unto you my gospel, and this is the gospel which I have given unto you—that I came into the world to do the will of my Father, because my Father sent me. And my Father sent me that I might be lifted up upon the cross; and after that I had been lifted up upon the cross, that I might draw all men unto me, that as I have been lifted up by men even so should men be lifted up by the Father, to stand before me, to be judged of their works, whether they be good or whether they be evil (3 Nephi 27:13–14).

All the prophets of old, whether in the Old Testament, New Testament, or Book of Mormon, use similar phrases in describing our redemption by Jesus Christ. Some speak of reconciliation with Christ, others speak of His intercession for our sins, and still others emphasize His deliverance and grace. But there is one expression in the song of redeeming love reserved alone for the Savior Himself, and that is, "Come unto me" (Matthew 11:28).

Just as Samuel the Lamanite had prophesied thirty-eight years previously, the Nephites in the western hemisphere did,

167

indeed, experience great geological upheavals followed by three days of darkness, signifying the crucifixion of Christ half a world away. Suddenly, the darkness was penetrated by a voice from on high recounting the massive destruction of various great cities. The Savior's voice explained that the survivors had been spared because of their righteousness relative to those who perished. He then asked them: "Will ye not now *return unto me*, and repent of your sins, and be converted, that I may heal you?" And again the invitation: "Yea, verily I say unto you, if ye will *come unto me* ye shall have eternal life. Behold, mine arm of mercy is extended towards you, and whosoever will come, him will I receive; and blessed are those who *come unto me*" (3 Nephi 9:13–14; emphasis added).

He then testified: "I am Jesus Christ the Son of God. I created the heavens and the earth, and all things that in them are. . . . I have come unto the world to bring redemption unto the world, to save the world from sin. Therefore, whoso repenteth and *cometh unto me* as a little child, him will I receive, for of such is the kingdom of God. Behold, for such I have laid down my life, and have taken it up again; therefore repent, and *come unto me* ye ends of the earth, and be saved" (3 Nephi 9:15, 21–22; emphasis added).

This invitation is universally extended to everyone who has lived, now lives, or will yet live on the earth, regardless of nationality, socioeconomic status, ethnic background, age, race, or gender.

As a great multitude of people gathered at the temple in Bountiful, they again heard a voice from the heavens: "It was not a harsh voice, neither was it a loud voice; nevertheless, and notwithstanding it being a small voice it did pierce them that did hear to the center, . . . and did cause their hearts to burn." The Father then introduced His Only Begotten Son: "Behold my Beloved Son, in whom I am well pleased, in whom I have glorified my name—hear ye him" (3 Nephi 11:3, 7).

The Savior of the world descended from heaven clothed in a pure white robe and walked among the Nephites, who fell to the earth in His presence. He bade them to "arise and *come forth unto me*, that ye may thrust your hands into my side, and also that ye may feel the prints of the nails in my hands and in my feet, that ye may know that I am the God of Israel, and the God of the whole earth, and have been slain for the sins of the world" (3 Nephi 11:14; emphasis added). There could hardly be a greater confirmation of Christ's role as our personal Savior than His intimate invitation for each individual to come forward and physically handle the scars of the wounds that had been inflicted upon Him in our behalf.

After calling the Twelve, the Savior gave the multitude what is known in the New Testament as the Sermon on the Mount. His New World Beatitudes were similar to those recorded in the Gospel of Matthew but contained a few significant additions. In Matthew we read, "Blessed are the poor in spirit: for theirs is the kingdom of heaven" (5:3). But to the ancient Nephites, He said, "Blessed are the poor in spirit *who come unto me*, for theirs is the kingdom of heaven" (3 Nephi 12:3; emphasis added). Countless inhabitants of the earth are poor in spirit: drug dealers, alcoholics, prostitutes, thieves, child abusers, liars, and those who hold a grudge or cannot forgive others of their offenses. The Savior's welcoming arms are open to all, but we must make the effort to come unto Him before we can be cleansed and healed.

The Savior's invitation has some conditions: "And behold, I have given you the law and the commandments of my Father, that ye shall believe in me, and that ye shall repent of your sins, and *come unto me* with a broken heart and a contrite spirit. . . . Therefore, *come unto me* and be ye saved; for verily I say unto you, that except ye shall keep my commandments . . . ye shall in no case enter into the kingdom of heaven" (3 Nephi 12:19–20; emphasis added).

He then prescribes some specific conditions under which we can become purified and made whole: "Therefore, if ye shall *come unto me*, or shall desire to *come unto me*, and remember-est that thy brother hath aught against thee—Go thy way unto thy brother, and first be reconciled to thy brother, and then *come unto me* with full purpose of heart, and I will receive you" (3 Nephi 12:23–24; emphasis added).

At the heart of the Atonement is the reconciliation between us sinners and Him whom our sins have offended. The Savior made it clear that His reconciliation with us depends upon our reconciliation with those around us. In latter-day revelation He said: "Ye ought to forgive one another; for he that forgiveth not his brother his trespasses standeth condemned before the Lord; for there remaineth in him the greater sin. I, the Lord, will for-give whom I will forgive, but of you it is required to forgive all men" (D&C 64:9–10).

Alma the Elder served as another witness to the indispens-ability of reconciliation when he taught the Saints of his day to "forgive one another your trespasses; for verily I say unto you, he that forgiveth not his neighbor's trespasses when he says that he repents, the same hath brought himself under condemna-tion" (Mosiah 26:31). There is a certain finality to Alma's coun-sel regarding the need for forgiveness and to the Savior's instruction to the Nephites and His revelations to the elders of the restored Church regarding the need for forgiveness. Little room exists for the excuse, "Yes, but you don't understand."

The mandate is not to forgive when it is easy or when the transgression involves others or when the infraction is financial rather than carnal in nature. Our forgiveness, like the rains from heaven, must fall upon the just and the unjust, those who deserve our compassion and those who do not.

The Savior taught the Nephites much of the content of the Sermon on the Mount and gave them the pattern of prayer, including the phrase, "And forgive us our debts, as we forgive our debtors." At the conclusion of the prayer, to ensure that his point was understood, the Lord taught, "If ye forgive men their trespasses your heavenly Father will also forgive you; but if ye forgive not men their trespasses neither will your Father forgive your trespasses" (3 Nephi 13:11, 14–15).

The Atonement is the miracle of forgiveness, and if we wish to claim that miracle, we too must forgive.

C. S. Lewis observed, "If you had a perfect excuse, you would not need forgiveness; if the whole of your action needs forgiveness, then there was no excuse for it. But the trouble is that what we call 'asking for God's forgiveness' very often really consists in asking God to accept our excuses."[1]

Thanks be to our loving Heavenly Father that our inexcusable actions are not, in his eyes, unforgivable.

The Lord taught the Nephites that the law of Moses was fulfilled in Him, and He told them of His other sheep, including those of scattered Israel. He tenderly healed their sick and afflicted, blessed their little children, and taught them the importance of the sacrament. He instructed His disciples that they should not allow the unworthy to partake of the sacrament, but He admonished them: "Nevertheless, ye shall not cast him out from among you, but . . . unto such shall ye continue to minister; for ye know not but what they will return and repent, and *come unto me* with full purpose of heart, and I shall heal them; and ye shall be the means of bringing salvation unto them" (3 Nephi 18:30–32; emphasis added). The requirements are rigorous, but the Savior lovingly taught His disciples to keep the door ajar for the laggards and latecomers.

The late group includes the scattered remnant of Israel. The Savior told the Nephites: "I will remember the covenant which I have made with my people; and I have covenanted with them that I would gather them together in mine own due time, that I would give unto them again the land of their fathers for their inheritance, which is the land of Jerusalem, which is the promised land unto them forever, saith the Father" (3 Nephi 20:29).

The Lord extended a hopeful, yet conditional, prophecy that as the works of righteousness reach the Gentiles, "if they will not harden their hearts, . . . they may repent and *come unto me* and be baptized in my name and know of the true points of my doctrine, that they may be numbered among my people, O house of Israel" (3 Nephi 21:6; emphasis added). As was His practice in the Holy Land, the Savior quoted Isaiah at some length and admonished the people to "search these things diligently; for great are the words of Isaiah" (3 Nephi 22, 23:1).

Although the Nephites had access to Isaiah's words, their forebears had left Jerusalem prior to the time of the prophet Malachi. The Savior, therefore, provided them with Malachi's teachings on tithing, preparation for the Second Coming, and Elijah's mission to turn "the heart of the fathers to the children, and the heart of the children to their fathers" (3 Nephi 24, 25:5–6).

While I was serving as a mission president in Vienna, Austria, we occasionally held Sunday evening firesides in the mission home. At the conclusion of a fireside one March, I had a pleasant chat with a bright young man named Michael Dimmel. In his mid-twenties, Michael was working as a computer programmer and had shown a sincere interest in the Church. Before he left for home, I asked him, "Michael, when will you be ready to be baptized a member of this Church?" He replied, "I'm not sure. Certainly not before October." I asked in amazement, "October? The Second Coming is in July. Surely you cannot wait that long!" With a smile, he said, "We'll see." Then he left.

A couple of days later, I received a phone call. "This is Michael. You told me the other evening that if I had any questions I could call you. May I come see you?" I was only too happy to welcome him to my office.

He began the conversation somewhat falteringly. "Herr President," he said, "the missionaries told me that if I would read the Book of Mormon and pray about it I would know it was true and I would have a desire to be baptized. Now, Herr President, please do not be angry with me, but I have started to read the Book and, please forgive me, but I think the Book of Mormon is drier than reading the Vienna telephone directory."

I felt prompted to say, "Michael, in your case, maybe you started in the wrong spot. Perhaps it would be better if we started somewhere in the middle, say 3 Nephi 17. Maybe I could read a few verses and then you could read a few verses." And so I started to read.

"Behold, now it came to pass that when Jesus had spoken these words he looked round about again on the multitude, and he said unto them: Behold, my time is at hand.

"I perceive that ye are weak, that ye cannot understand all my words which I am commanded of the Father to speak unto you at this time.

"Therefore, go ye unto your homes, and ponder upon the things which I have said, and ask of the Father, in my name, that ye may understand, and prepare your minds for the morrow, and I come unto you again.

"But now I go unto the Father, and also to show myself unto the lost tribes of Israel, for they are not lost unto the Father, for he knoweth whither he hath taken them.

"And it came to pass that when Jesus had thus spoken, he cast his eyes round about again on the multitude, and beheld they were in tears, and did look steadfastly upon him as if they would ask him to tarry a little longer with them.

"And he said unto them: Behold, my bowels are filled with compassion towards you. Have ye any that are sick among you? Bring them hither. Have ye any that are lame, or blind, or halt, or maimed, or leprous, or that are withered, or that are deaf, or that are afflicted in any manner? Bring them hither and I will heal them, for I have compassion upon you; my bowels are filled with mercy.

"For I perceive that ye desire that I should show unto you what I have done unto your brethren at Jerusalem, for I see that your faith is sufficient that I should heal you.

"And it came to pass that when he had thus spoken, all the multitude, with one accord, did go forth with their sick and their afflicted, and their lame, and with their blind, and with their dumb, and with all them that were afflicted in any manner; and he did heal them every one as they were brought forth unto him.

"And they did all, both they who had been healed and they who were whole, bow down at his feet, and did worship him; and as many as could come for the multitude did kiss his feet, insomuch that they did bathe his feet with their tears" (3 Nephi 17:1–10).

I suggested that Michael then take a turn and read a few verses.

"And it came to pass that he commanded that their little children should be brought. So they brought their little children and set them down upon the ground round about him, and Jesus stood in the midst; and the multitude gave way till they had all been brought unto him.

"And it came to pass that when they had all been brought, and Jesus stood in the midst, he commanded the multitude that they should kneel down upon the ground.

"And it came to pass that when they had knelt upon the ground, Jesus groaned within himself, and said: Father, I am troubled because of the wickedness of the people of the house of Israel.

"And when he had said these words, he himself also knelt upon the earth; and behold he prayed unto the Father, and the things which he prayed cannot be written, and the multitude did bear record who heard him.

"And after this manner do they bear record: The eye hath never seen, neither hath the ear heard, before, so great and marvelous things as we saw and heard Jesus speak unto the Father;

"And no tongue can speak, neither can there be written by any man, neither can the hearts of men conceive so great and marvelous things as we both saw and heard Jesus speak; and no one can conceive of the joy which filled our souls at the time we heard him pray for us unto the Father.

"And it came to pass that when Jesus had made an end of praying unto the Father, he arose; but so great was the joy of the multitude that they were overcome.

"And it came to pass that Jesus spake unto them, and bade them arise. And they arose from the earth, and he said unto them: Blessed are ye because of your faith. And now behold, my joy is full.

"And when he had said these words, he wept, and the multitude bare record of it, and he took their little children, one by one, and blessed them, and prayed unto the Father for them. And when he had done this he wept again" (3 Nephi 17:11–22).

As Michael read, his voice began to crack, and as he cleared his throat, I realized he was experiencing some feelings he had never felt before. As the Spirit tripped his emotional circuit breakers, tears flowed gently down his cheeks. He suggested that I read a few more verses.

"And he spake unto the multitude, and said unto them: Behold your little ones. And as they looked to behold they cast their eyes towards heaven, and they saw the heavens open, and they saw angels descending out of heaven as it were in the midst of fire; and they came down and encircled those little ones about, and they were encircled about with fire; and the angels did minister unto them.

"And the multitude did see and hear and bear record; and they know that their record is true for they all of them did see and hear, every man for himself; and they were in number about two thousand and five hundred souls; and they did consist of men, women, and children" (3 Nephi 17:23–25).

We closed our books and just sat there for a minute of silent introspection, basking in the Spirit, which we had felt during the reading of this powerful chapter. Finally Michael broke the silence, "I'm going home to read the whole Book of Mormon," he said with firm conviction. He had just experienced what Lehi had experienced two thousand six hundred years previously: "And it came to pass that as he read, he was filled with the Spirit of the Lord" (1 Nephi 1:12).

I am pleased to report that Michael was baptized a couple of weeks later on Easter Sunday. Such is the spirit and converting power of the Book of Mormon.

LIFTING

As the time drew near for the Savior to depart from the Nephites, He taught them that His Church should bear His name, and then He left them with a profound and succinct definition of the very essence of His gospel:

"Behold I have given unto you my gospel, and this is the

gospel which I have given unto you—that I came into the world to do the will of my Father, because my Father sent me.

"And my Father sent me that I might be *lifted* up upon the cross; and after that I had been *lifted* up upon the cross, that I might draw all men unto me, that as I have been *lifted* up by men even so should men be *lifted* up by the Father, to stand before me, to be judged of their works, whether they be good or whether they be evil—

"And for this cause have I been *lifted* up; therefore, according to the power of the Father I will draw all men unto me, that they may be judged according to their works.

"Now this is the commandment: Repent, all ye ends of the earth, and *come unto me* and be baptized in my name, that ye may be sanctified by the reception of the Holy Ghost, that ye may stand spotless before me at the last day.

"Verily, verily, I say unto you, this is my gospel; and ye know the things that ye must do in my church; for the works which ye have seen me do that shall ye also do; for that which ye have seen me do even that shall ye do" (3 Nephi 27:13–15; 20–21; emphasis added).

NOTE

1. Lewis, *The Weight of Glory,* 122.

SIXTEEN

Isaiah's Song of Comfort

Sing, O heavens; and be joyful, O earth; for the feet of those who are in the east shall be established; and break forth into singing, O mountains; for they shall be smitten no more; for the Lord hath comforted his people, and will have mercy upon his afflicted (1 Nephi 21:13).

When Lehi's sons returned with the brass plates they had obtained from Laban, they learned that they contained "a record of the Jews from the beginning, even down to the commencement of the reign of Zedekiah, king of Judah" in approximately 598 B.C. (1 Nephi 5:12). Among the writings of Old Testament prophets found on the plates were those of Isaiah, which were quoted at length by Nephi, Jacob, Abinadi, and the Savior Himself during His visit to the ancient Nephites.

Because of Isaiah's prolific use of symbolic metaphors, Nephi acknowledged to his people that "the words of Isaiah are not plain unto you, nevertheless they are plain unto all those that are filled with the spirit of prophecy." Nephi then proclaimed, "My soul delighteth in the words of Isaiah" (2 Nephi 25:4–5). During the Savior's visit to the Nephites, He commanded the people to search the scriptures, "for great are the words of Isaiah. For surely he spake as touching all things concerning my people which are of the house of Israel" (3 Nephi 23:1–2).

Throughout all his writings we hear the song of redeeming love as he focuses upon the Savior's birth, His mortal ministry in healing the downtrodden, His atoning sacrifice, and His concern with gathering the wayward house of Israel. The Book of Mormon contains 433 verses from Isaiah's writings, roughly equivalent to thirty-five of its pages.

FORGIVENESS

Isaiah's record begins with a solemn reminder that the Lord wearies of animal sacrifices and desires that we wash and cleanse ourselves, put away our evil doings, and "learn to do well" (Isaiah 1:11–17). He then extends a loving invitation: "Come now, and let us reason together, saith the Lord: though your sins be as scarlet, they shall be as white as snow; though they be red like crimson, they shall be as wool" (Isaiah 1:18).

I have seen men and women sob uncontrollably with tears of joy as I have referred to this scripture in a special baptismal interview or during the restoration of temple blessings. Isaiah's eloquent metaphors contain great power because his use of symbols allows more to be caught than was taught. The juxtaposition of the imagery of "scarlet sins" and pure "white snow" is a convincing confirmation of cleansing from sin. When Isaiah contrasts crimson and wool, he tacitly reminds us that the blood of the Lamb of God will cleanse the garments of those who repent of their sins (1 Nephi 12:10; Alma 5:21; 13:11; 3 Nephi 27:19).

It would be difficult to find a more graphic example of scarlet sins becoming as white as snow than in the lives of Alma the Younger and the four sons of Mosiah. Prior to their dramatic conversion, these young lads were described as "the very vilest of sinners. And the Lord saw fit in his infinite mercy to spare them; nevertheless they suffered much anguish of soul because of their iniquities, suffering much and fearing that they should be cast off forever" (Mosiah 28:4).

More than two decades after the angel appeared to them, Alma the Younger recounted that he had "murdered many of [God's] children, or rather led them away unto destruction" (Alma 36:14).

When Mormon wished to convey the capability of Captain Moroni's righteous leadership, he wrote: "If all men had been, and were, and ever would be, like unto Moroni, behold, the very powers of hell would have been shaken forever; yea, the devil would never have power over the hearts of the children of men. Behold, he was a man like unto Ammon, the son of Mosiah, yea, and even the other sons of Mosiah, yea, and also Alma and his sons, for they were all men of God" (Alma 48:17–18). Alma, Ammon, Aaron, Omner, and Himni had undergone a mighty change of heart from being "the vilest of sinners" to becoming "men of God." Though their sins were as crimson, they had become as white as wool.

After rebuking the Israelites for wearying Him with their iniquities, the Lord, through Isaiah, spoke these words of comforting assurance: "I, even I, am he that blotteth out thy transgressions for mine own sake, and will not remember thy sins. Put me in remembrance" (Isaiah 43:25–26). He assures those of the house of Israel that he has not forgotten them and that "I have blotted out, as a thick cloud, thy transgressions, and, as a cloud, thy sins: return unto me; for I have redeemed thee. Sing, O ye heavens; for the Lord hath done it: shout, ye lower parts of the earth: break forth into singing, ye mountains, O forest, and every tree therein: for the Lord hath redeemed Jacob, and glorified himself in Israel" (Isaiah 44:22–23).

Abinadi cited Isaiah at length while testifying to King Noah and his wicked priests of the Savior's atoning sacrifice:

"For he shall grow up before him as a tender plant, and as a root out of dry ground; he hath no form nor comeliness; and when we shall see him there is no beauty that we should desire him.

"He is despised and rejected of men; a man of sorrows, and acquainted with grief; and we hid as it were our faces from him; he was despised, and we esteemed him not.

"Surely he has borne our griefs, and carried our sorrows; yet we did esteem him stricken, smitten of God, and afflicted. But he was wounded for our transgressions, he was bruised for our iniquities; the chastisement of our peace was upon him; and with his stripes we are healed.

"All we, like sheep, have gone astray; we have turned every one to his own way; and the Lord hath laid on him the iniquities of us all. . . . Therefore will I divide him a portion with the great, and he shall divide the spoil with the strong; because he hath *poured out his soul unto death*; and he was numbered with the transgressors; and he bore the sins of many, and made intercession for the transgressors" (Mosiah 14:2–6, 12; emphasis added).

The Savior poured out His soul that He might drink all of the bitter cup, paying for my sins, your sins, and the sins of all those who have lived or will yet live in the world. His suffering caused Him to bleed at every pore, and because He emptied His soul unto death, He had power to empty the garden tomb, being filled with immortality and the glory of the Father. Willingly sinking to the ultimate depths allowed Him to rise to glorious heights "with healing in His wings" (3 Nephi 25:2).

HEALING

Isaiah succinctly summarized the consequences of the Savior's Atonement: "He will swallow up death in victory; and the Lord God will wipe away tears from off all faces" (Isaiah

25:8). As wondrous as the promise is that "He will swallow up death in victory," the wonder of the infinite Atonement is magnified by the additional promise that "the Lord God will wipe away tears from off all faces."

He suffered for the sins of all who have lived or will yet live upon this earth "that they might not suffer if they would repent; but if they would not repent, they must suffer even as I; which suffering caused myself, even God, the greatest of all, to tremble because of pain, and to bleed at every pore, and to suffer both body and spirit" (D&C 19:16–18).

He will wipe away all the tears from all the faces of those who repent and come unto Him, regardless of the source of their tears. The wife whose philandering husband broke her heart will, with that broken heart and contrite spirit, have her tears dried by a gentle hand whose warmth will kindle flames of forgiveness. Victims of child abuse will have their tears dried by Him who declared that He is their spiritual Father, and if they will be "steadfast and immovable, always abounding in good works, . . . Christ . . . will seal them His" (Mosiah 5:7, 15). The tears of loneliness of those who have lost marriage companions or who never had an opportunity to marry will also be wiped away. "I will not leave you comfortless," is His eternal promise (John 14:18).

He will dry all the tears from all the faces of those who spent their mortal existence trying to hold a steady job but failed, of those who tried to be good parents but failed, and of those who tried to please their parents but failed. To each and all of these, "the work of righteousness shall be peace; and the effect of righteousness quietness and assurance for ever. And my people shall dwell in a peaceable habitation, and in sure dwellings, and in quiet resting places" (Isaiah 32:17–18), where His peace passes all human understanding (Philippians 4:7).

His song of redeeming love will be heard throughout the

universe: "Sing, O heavens; and be joyful, O earth; and break forth into singing, O mountains: for the Lord hath comforted his people, and will have mercy upon his afflicted" (Isaiah 49:13).

For those who feel oppressed, who carry heavy burdens, or who are in bondage of any kind, the Lord provides a means of escape: "Is not this the fast that I have chosen? To loose the bands of wickedness, to undo the heavy burdens, and to let the oppressed go free, and that ye break every yoke?" (Isaiah 58:6). When we come to the Lord in fervent prayer and fasting, He will bless us in our emptiness with the fulness of His gospel and the fulness of His love. As we subject our bodies to our spirit, He will loose the bands of addiction and lift our burdens that they may be light. He will help us escape from all forms of oppression, including unpleasant memories. He will break every yoke that may impede our spiritual progress. We can then take His yoke upon us, for His yoke is easy and His burden is light (Matthew 11:29–30).

Speaking messianically, Isaiah concluded his writing by eloquently encapsulating the Savior's entire ministry: "The Spirit of the Lord God is upon me; because the Lord hath anointed me to preach good tidings unto the meek; he hath sent me to bind up the brokenhearted, to proclaim liberty to the captives, and the opening of the prison to them that are bound . . . to comfort all that mourn . . . to give unto them beauty for ashes, the oil of joy for mourning, the garment of praise for the spirit of heaviness; that they might be called trees of righteousness, the planting of the Lord, that he might be glorified" (Isaiah 61:1–3).

GATHERING

Isaiah directed much of his attention to the scattered house of Israel, assuring that "the Lord shall set his hand again the second time to recover the remnant of his people. . . . And he shall set up an ensign for the nations, and shall assemble the outcasts of Israel" (Isaiah 11:11–12; 2 Nephi 21:11–12).

Because the Lord used Isaiah as His mouthpiece, Isaiah frequently spoke in the first person as if the Lord's message were his own. The Lord uses varied imagery to capture the attention of wayward Israel, such as comparing Himself to the loving mother whose wayward children have forgotten and forsaken her. The Lord plucked at their very heartstrings when He asked, "Can a woman forget her sucking child, that she should not have compassion on the son of her womb? Yea, they may forget, yet will I not forget thee." Then, in an allusion to His allowing evil men to drive spikes through His hands, He declared, "Behold, I have graven thee upon the palms of my hands" (Isaiah 49:14–16) Because He died for all the sins of all of us, He quite literally engraved our names upon the palms of His hands.

On another occasion He compared Himself to the bridegroom whose wife has been unfaithful, but then He asks, "Where is the bill of your mother's divorcement, whom I have put away? . . . Is my hand shortened at all, that it cannot redeem? Or have I no power to deliver?" In other words, the Lord assured the children of Israel that He is going to keep His covenant with them even if they occasionally forget their covenant with Him (Isaiah 50:1–2). "For a small moment have I forsaken thee; but with great mercies will I gather thee," and "the ransomed of the Lord shall return, and come to Zion with songs and everlasting joy" (Isaiah 54:7; 35:10).

The Savior's infinite atonement will become accessible to everyone who has ever lived or who will yet live upon this earth. All will be resurrected regardless of their degree of obedience or disobedience, for the promise is sure that "as in Adam all die, even so in Christ shall all be made alive"

(1 Corinthians 15:22). Salvation from physical death is a gift given freely to all. However, exaltation in the presence of God requires us to exercise our faith in Christ, repent of our sins, be baptized for a remission of our sins, and receive the gift of the Holy Ghost through the laying on of hands. Exaltation in the celestial kingdom requires that we receive our temple endowment and be sealed to a companion for time and eternity.

Latter-day Saints are members of the only true and living Church (D&C 1:30), the leaders of which hold priesthood keys to administer the ordinances of the gospel required for exaltation. Nevertheless, members of The Church of Jesus Christ of Latter-day Saints have no monopoly on the miracle of forgiveness or the blessings and comfort that accrue to anyone who forgives others.

FORGIVENESS

Edith Taylor was not a member of the Church, but she understood well the Savior's injunction: "For, if ye forgive men their trespasses your heavenly Father will also forgive you; but if ye forgive not men their trespasses neither will your Father forgive your trespasses" (3 Nephi 13:14–15; Matthew 6:14–15). If her life story had been a movie script, the critics would have panned it for being too unrealistic and unbelievable. That is because her story is one of unflinching devotion and boundless love and forgiveness, which inoculated her broken heart against feelings of retribution and bitterness.

Edith had been happily married to her husband, Karl, for twenty-three years. Karl was employed in a government warehouse in Waltham, Massachusetts. His job required no traveling and allowed him to be home every night. But in February of 1950, everything changed when Karl was sent overseas to work for the government in a new warehouse in Okinawa.

The original plan called for Karl to be away for just a few

months, but he wrote to explain that his assignment had been extended for a couple of weeks. Later he wrote that his extension would last another month or two. Then came the bombshell: "Dear Edith. I wish there were a kinder way to tell you that we are no longer married." Edith was stunned to learn that Karl had written to Mexico for a "mail-order divorce." He had done so in order to marry Aiko, his nineteen-year-old Japanese maid.

Edith could have contested such a flimsy divorce. She also could have spent the rest of her life telling anyone who would listen of the cruel treatment she had received at the hands of her unfaithful husband. But after twenty-three years of marriage Edith simply could not find it in her soul to hate Karl. She imagined that he had missed her just as she had missed him. He had longed for physical affection, and the teenaged maid was close at hand. She decided that he thought he had done the honorable thing by divorcing her to make his relationship with Aiko open and aboveboard.

After marshaling her inner strength, Edith wrote to Karl, suggesting that he let her know what was happening in his life. So he did. He wrote about the birth of their baby, Maria, in 1951 and the subsequent birth of Helen two years later. Karl's letters allowed her to track the growth of these little girls. Then came a second bombshell: Karl informed her that he had been diagnosed with terminal lung cancer. He was fearful for the future of his little girls. He had hoped to send them to America someday, but his medical bills had depleted all his funds.

To give Karl peace of mind, Edith offered to take the two little girls and rear them in Waltham. After considerable resistance, but realizing that their life in Okinawa would be one of poverty, Aiko sent them to their "Aunt Edith" in November 1956. Though caring for such little ones was a challenge, Edith confessed that it was fun to fix meals again and a joy to see the little girls develop a happy, well-fed look.

Aiko sent letters in broken English, asking about her daughters, explaining how much she missed them. Edith eventually realized that Aiko belonged with her children, but the immigration waiting list for Japanese citizens was extremely long. Edith appealed to the news media for assistance, and in response to her pleas, Aiko was able to come to America in 1957. As the plane approached the airport in New York City, Edith had a surge of fear that she might perhaps hate this young woman who had stolen away her husband. But as she observed a frail little Japanese immigrant mother disembark from the plane with a face filled with apprehension, all of Edith's fears vanished. After recognizing Edith, Aiko ran into her open arms, and they held each other tightly for a long time.

"I prayed for Karl to come back," Edith thought. "Now he has—in his two little daughters and in this gentle girl he loved. Help me, God, to love her too." After the passage of several years, Edith wrote of her experiences:

"Though God has taken one life I loved dearly, He has given me three others to love. I am so thankful."[1]

NOTE

1. Bob Considine, "Could You Have Loved as Much?" *Reader's Digest,* April 1966, 73–75.

SEVENTEEN

Mormon's Song of Miracles

And he hath brought to pass the redemption of the world, whereby he that is found guiltless before him at the judgment day hath it given unto him to dwell in the presence of God in his kingdom, to sing ceaseless praises with the choirs above, unto the Father, and unto the Son, and unto the Holy Ghost, which are one God, in a state of happiness which hath no end (Mormon 7:7).

Joseph Smith and Oliver Cowdery were in the process of translating the Book of Mormon when they encountered a passage dealing with baptism. The Book of Mormon up to that point had not explained how one should be baptized nor by what authority. Joseph and Oliver retired to the banks of the Susquehanna River, where they queried the Lord regarding these two questions. In response to their faithful, humble prayer, the resurrected John the Baptist appeared to them. He laid his hands upon their heads and said, "Upon you my fellow servants, in the name of Messiah I confer the Priesthood of Aaron, which holds the keys of the ministering of angels" (D&C 13).

Ministering angels have been, and continue to be, an essential part of the restoration of the gospel in the dispensation of the fulness of times. The Lord revealed that the Book of Mormon "was given by inspiration, and is confirmed to others by the ministering of angels, and is declared unto the world by them—proving to the world that the holy scriptures are true" (D&C 20:10–11).

Several years ago President Robert Peterson of the Germany Hamburg Mission called me one morning to tell me about two of his missionaries who had been teaching a young man from Lebanon. This investigator had expressed some interest in learning more about the gospel, but after the second discussion it became apparent that his interest was superficial because he failed to accept the invitation to read the Book of Mormon. He indicated to the elders that there was little need in his life for an additional holy book. The missionaries told him they would no longer be visiting him because he was so resistant to their challenge to read the Book of Mormon, and they crossed him off their list of active investigators.

That night this young Lebanese fellow had an interesting dream. He dreamed that he was walking along the bank of a very large river. The riverbank was quite different from any other he had seen before because there was some kind of metal banister along the path. It seemed the banister had been put there to prevent people from falling into the river. As he walked along the path, he was suddenly enveloped by a thick bank of fog. Fearing that he would lose his way and possibly fall into the river, he grabbed hold of the metal railing for dear life.

As he continued through the mist of darkness, he suddenly saw at the end of the path a tree adorned with beautiful white fruit. As he approached the tree, he partook of the fruit. It was delicious, so he took a second piece of fruit, finding it even more delicious than the first. Then he heard a voice in his dream say distinctly, "Be baptized."

The next morning when he awoke, he recalled in vivid

detail his dream. He hurriedly dressed and went out to look for the missionaries. Fortunately, they were going door to door a couple of blocks from where he lived. When he spotted them on the street, he yelled loudly, "Elders! I want to be baptized." That got their attention, and they immediately repented of having crossed him off their list the previous evening.

As he ran toward the elders, this young man, in an animated voice, recounted the dream of the previous evening. When he finished relating his dream, one of the elders said, "Oh, so you've already begun reading the Book of Mormon." He said, "No, I haven't begun reading it yet, but I *will* read it." The other elder then opened his Book of Mormon to 1 Nephi 8. The young Lebanese man read the chapter carefully, and then he said, "That's my dream!" One of the missionaries rejoined, "But Lehi had it first."

The Lord calls upon His children by the ministering of angels (D&C 43:25). But because the hollowing precedes the hallowing, some of the Lord's modern-day servants were told that they were not able to abide the ministering of angels until they humbled themselves and stripped themselves of fears and jealousies (D&C 67:10, 13).

The prophet Mormon, speaking of the ministering of angels, asked, "Have miracles ceased?" He then answered his own question: "Behold I say unto you, Nay; neither have angels ceased to minister unto the children of men," for "it is by faith that miracles are wrought; and it is by faith that angels appear and minister unto men" (Moroni 7:29, 37).

After their dramatic conversion, Alma and the sons of Mosiah dedicated their lives to preaching the gospel, for "they could not bear that any human soul should perish" (Mosiah 28:3). Alma was called to the city of Ammonihah, but the people rejected him and cast him out. In his tribulation, an angel appeared unto him. This angel identified himself as the same angel who had appeared earlier in response to the prayers of Alma's father (Alma 8:13–15; Mosiah 27:13–15). This messenger of the Lord instructed Alma to return to Ammonihah, where he met Amulek (Alma 8:18–20). This is one way ministering angels assist in missionary work. They give missionaries a nudge to go in a certain direction, and they guide other people to come toward the missionaries. When missionaries are in tune with the Spirit, they become powerful tools in finding people to teach.

THE GOSPEL IN GREECE

Greece is a very tradition-bound country, and it is a perpetual challenge there to find people to teach. Elder David Nelson and his companion, Elder Shawn Stephens, had been laboring with all their heart, might, mind, and strength to find people to teach in Athens. They had visited the members to solicit referrals, they had contacted people on the streets, and they had invested considerable time and energy in going door to door. They returned to their apartment one day and poured out their hearts to the Lord. They pleaded with Him to help them find someone to teach in that city of five million people. In meekness, these two humble elders told the Lord they would be in the Brazil Square park that afternoon between three and five, and they would be grateful if He would prompt someone interested in the gospel to be in the park during those hours.

At about the same time the elders arose from prayer, a native Athenian named Louvaris was heading for home on a bus. He had ridden that same bus at that same time each day for several years. But on this particular afternoon the thought entered his mind that although he had lived in Athens his entire life, he had never visited the park at Brazil Square, which was located on his bus route. He recalled:

"It was a summer afternoon on July 27, 1989, and it appears that the hand of God guided me to the true Church. While I was coming from my work toward my house, wholly unexpectedly, I got off the trolley two stops before the usual stop.

"I was at a loss! I walked about 100 meters in perplexity, and then I thought of going to the park [at Brazil Square] to sit a while on the bench, even though the time was 2:45 P.M. and it was very hot.

"And so I did. I like to sit by myself in parks and think and reflect. Certainly the hour was unsuitable, but a power was urging me to do it.

"I sat thinking and reflecting for about seven minutes, and suddenly I saw before me two well-dressed young men holding some white flyers in their hands. I thought that they were heaven-sent. The one was very tall (Elder Nelson), and the second was shorter (Elder Stephens).

"They immediately gave me a flyer. I read it and discovered that they were missionaries from the Church of Jesus Christ of Latter-day Saints. They were Mormons. The content of the flyer concerned me very much. It read, 'How to Make a Happy Family.'

"The missionaries, seeing my interest in knowing them and their Church, suggested that I go at that moment to visit their Church. Miraculously, it was located just across from us!

"I felt the presence of God near me. I accepted with joy and we went immediately. They showed me a video about the Prophet Joseph Smith. I liked it very much. But the thing I will not ever forget was the simplicity of the missionaries, their continual smiles, the light in their faces, and, above all, the joy with which they surrounded me. I felt that I had known them for a long time.

"We set up two meetings a week at my house. They were,

indeed, edifying discussions. The Spirit of God was strong, and the hand of God helped me. He took me and showed me the correct road, the road that leads toward Him and His glory.

"At last I was ready to be baptized. I knew what baptism meant. I knew that I was reborn, that I had made a covenant with God to serve Him faithfully until the end in order to be saved."[1]

Brother Louvaris later became the president of the Athens Branch.

MINISTERING ANGELS

Who are these angels who assist in the work of the Lord? The Lord has revealed that "there are no angels who minister to this earth but those who do belong or have belonged to it" (D&C 130:5). President Joseph F. Smith gave us some additional insight: "When messengers are sent to minister to the inhabitants of this earth, they are not strangers, but from the ranks of our kindred, friends, and fellow-beings and fellow-servants. . . . Our fathers and mothers, brothers, sisters and friends who have passed away from this earth . . . may have a mission given them to visit their relatives and friends upon the earth again, bringing from the divine Presence messages of love, of warning, or reproof and instruction, to those whom they had learned to love in the flesh."[2]

It is well to note that, although ministering angels will accompany us and help us, we must still do the work. For example, the angel directed Alma into the path of Amulek, but the angel did not call Amulek on a mission. That was Alma's task. President Joseph Fielding Smith taught us that "it is contrary to the law of God for the heavens to be opened and messengers to come to do anything for man that man can do for himself."[3]

Ministering angels may guide missionaries into a given

neighborhood, but they will not knock on the doors for them. In Acts 10, we learn of a devout Italian centurion named Cornelius who, in response to his prayers, was visited by an angel. The angel told him to send for a man named Simon Peter in the city of Joppa. Thereafter it was Peter, not the angel, who taught Cornelius and his family the gospel (vv. 19–48).[4]

Elder Neal A. Maxwell has observed that "in the economy of heaven, God does not send thunder if a still, small voice is enough, or a prophet if a priest can do the job."[5]

A PRIESTHOOD BLESSING

Nearly two decades ago I had the privilege of serving as a stake president of one of the Brigham Young University student stakes. A member of our stake Relief Society presidency was a lovely, energetic woman in her mid-sixties who radiated the spirit of the gospel wherever she went. She had a positive influence on the young women in our stake, and it was a privilege to work with her. One day I received a shocking phone call, informing me that her husband had suffered a massive heart attack. A few days later he passed away. Her sorrow at the passing of her husband was magnified by the fact that they had planned to serve a mission together, and now that would not be possible in this life. Notwithstanding the sudden separation from her eternal companion, she continued to exude a spirit of hope and optimism and served as a source of inspiration to us all.

Several days after her husband's passing, she called to ask if I would come to her home and give her a priesthood blessing of comfort in her time of bereavement. I was honored to do so and took one of my counselors to assist me. As we entered her living room I noticed a small portable tape recorder on an end table near the couch. The thought occurred to me that she was going to ask if it was all right to record the priesthood blessing that we were about to give her. I would have to tell her that the *General Handbook of Instructions* states that patriarchal blessings are to be recorded and submitted to the Church Historical Department and that a father's blessing may be recorded and kept at home as a private family record. But other blessings, such as the setting apart of a missionary or a blessing of comfort, are not to be tape-recorded, as a general rule.

After we inquired about her situation and how she was dealing with the loneliness associated with her husband's departure, she asked if we would proceed with a blessing. Just as I anticipated, she asked, "Would it be okay to record the blessing so I could play it from time to time?" I knew my counselor did everything by the book, so I was quite confident he would give her the appropriate response. I turned to him and asked, "What do you think?" He smiled, looked at her and said, "Under these circumstances I think recording the blessing would be a great source of comfort to you." Well, what could I say?

We placed our hands upon the head of this pure sister who had been so faithful to her covenants and callings in the Church, and the words of the blessing flowed freely. At the conclusion of the blessing we bid her adieu, comforted by the absolute knowledge that a loving Heavenly Father knew who she was and where she was and what she needed most.

We continued to visit this sister from time to time, but no one made reference to the content of the blessing. Then, one morning, as I was working in my office, the phone rang. The voice was familiar. "Nine months ago you gave me a special priesthood blessing of comfort and direction. I have listened to the recording of that blessing every day for the past nine months and have it memorized. In that blessing you promised me that in the near future I would meet another man and that we would marry and eventually serve a mission together."

Measuring my words carefully, I responded, "Yes, I vaguely remember those promises."

"Well," she asked somewhat abruptly, "where is he?"

My heart sank. Now I knew why we are generally counseled not to record certain blessings. I stumbled for words. "Dear sister, I will counsel with the Lord and call you back."

I dropped to my knees at my desk and implored the Lord to give me some direction. This dear, faithful sister had placed her confidence in her priesthood leaders and we had been prompted to make certain promises. Now she merely wanted to know if the Lord was still interested in her. As I rose from prayer, I had a sudden flash of inspiration: "Call Sandy Bingham." My dear friend, Brother Sanford Bingham, was then serving as a counselor in the presidency of the Provo Temple. When I was a young bishop, he was on the stake high council and had often given me sage advice and counsel. "Have you thought about doing this or doing that to encourage your members to do more of this and less of that?" he would sometimes ask.

I called him at his office in the temple and said, "President Bingham, I'm in trouble and I need a ministering angel." I explained my predicament of pronouncing promises in the priesthood blessing that had not, as yet, come to fruition. I asked if he could give this matter some prayerful consideration and then call back.

The Lord works in mysterious ways His wonders to perform. There was a widower working in the Provo Temple whose wife had passed away at just about the same time our sister in the Relief Society presidency had lost her husband. Several months after this temple worker had lost his wife, President Bingham approached him in the temple one day and asked, "Dear brother, there are several widows working in the temple. How would you like me to introduce you to a few of them?" The widower gave President Bingham a rather curt response: "I loved my wife very much, and I am certainly not interested in meeting anyone else and remarrying."

That was in June. It was now November. President Bingham worked up his courage and once again approached this brother with the invitation to meet our stake Relief Society sister in his office. In order to be conciliatory with a member of the temple presidency, this good brother was agreeable. As nervous as two teenagers on their first date, the temple worker and the sister converged at President Bingham's office, where he graciously introduced them. Then, to their dismay, he excused himself and left them in his office alone together. Both were at a great loss for words, but finally the brother broke the silence and asked if he could take her to dinner the next evening. She readily agreed, and after confirming the appropriate details, they parted company.

Although the meeting in the temple had been a bit tense, the evening at the restaurant was an enjoyable occasion in a relaxed atmosphere in which two seemingly long lost friends became reacquainted. She liked to square dance and so did he. Their tastes in music and literature were similar, and both cheered for the same athletic teams. Their political preferences were also similar. She had always wanted to serve a mission with her husband, and he and his wife had also discussed the prospects of a mission together. And, of course, both had a great love for the temple and for their respective callings in the kingdom.

Three weeks after her fateful phone call, this dear sister called again, informing me that she and her newly found friend were engaged to be married a couple of months hence. They had been through temple sessions together, attended Church meetings together, square danced together, and been to various restaurants together, so why should they wait any longer? I sank to my knees in gratitude for an answer to prayer, and for ministering angels like President Bingham.

A few months after this marriage, I received yet another phone call. "We have some wonderful news to report, but we have to tell you in person," the newlyweds said. "Could you please drive over to see us this evening?" As my wife and I were driving to their home, Dorothea asked, "Do you have any idea what the important announcement is?" I replied, "I'm not sure, but at sixty-five, I don't think she's expecting."

As we arrived at our destination, the newlyweds opened the door wide. Before we could even enter their house they exclaimed jubilantly, "We received our mission call." Then, somewhat more subdued, she said, "Now all of the blessing has been fulfilled."

This could have been a sad story of two lonely individuals who lost their companions and spent the rest of their lives alone, but through the intervention of the Spirit and a ministering angel or two, they were brought together and became a great source of joy and companionship to each other and to others. But what of those who do not find companionship, either in their younger years or in their more mature years? The Savior's promise is still valid for all: "I will not leave you comfortless: I will come to you" (John 14:18). But if He is to come into our lives we must make room at the inn for Him by losing our lives in the service of others, by denying ourselves of all ungodliness, and by giving away all our sins to know Him (Matthew 10:39; Moroni 10:32; Alma 22:18).

If we will humble ourselves and draw near to our Heavenly Father in fasting and prayer on days when we feel hollow, our hollowness can make room for the fulness of gospel ordinances, covenants, and promised blessings of comfort and joy. "Have miracles ceased? Behold I say unto you, Nay; neither have angels ceased to minister unto the children of men" (Moroni 7:29).

THE MIRACLE OF FORGIVENESS

One of the greatest miracles of all is the miracle of being forgiven by a Father who loved us enough to give His Only Begotten Son as a ransom for our sins. The miracle of forgiveness also occurs when others forgive our offenses toward them and when we muster the strength to freely forgive them.

We are fortunate that Moroni included in his record his father's magnificent discourse on ministering angels, miracles, faith, hope and charity:

"And what is it that ye shall hope for? Behold I say unto you that ye shall have hope through the atonement of Christ and the power of his resurrection, to be raised unto life eternal, and this because of your faith in him according to the promise.

"Wherefore, if a man have faith he must needs have hope; for without faith there cannot be any hope. And again, behold I say unto you that he cannot have faith and hope, save he shall be meek, and lowly of heart.

"If so, his faith and hope is vain, for none is acceptable before God, save the meek and lowly in heart; and if a man be meek and lowly in heart, and confesses by the power of the Holy Ghost that Jesus is the Christ, he must needs have charity; for if he have not charity he is nothing; wherefore he must needs have charity.

"And charity suffereth long, and is kind, and envieth not, and is not puffed up, seeketh not her own, is not easily provoked, thinketh no evil, and rejoiceth not in iniquity but rejoiceth in the truth, beareth all things, believeth all things, hopeth all things, endureth all things.

"Wherefore, my beloved brethren, if ye have not charity, ye

are nothing, for charity never faileth. Wherefore, cleave unto charity, which is the greatest of all, for all things must fail—but charity is the pure love of Christ, and it endureth forever; and whoso is found possessed of it at the last day, it shall be well with him.

"Wherefore, my beloved brethren, pray unto the Father with all the energy of heart, that ye may be filled with this love, which he hath bestowed upon all who are true followers of his Son, Jesus Christ; that ye may become the sons of God; that when he shall appear we shall be like him, for we shall see him as he is; that we may have this hope; that we may be purified even as he is pure. Amen" (Moroni 7:41–48).

After defining charity as "the pure love of Christ," Mormon gives us a time-proven prescription for obtaining this love in our hearts. I recently received a letter from a lovely woman whose life was miraculously changed by the impact of Mormon's teachings. With her permission, I include some excerpts from her letter:

"I grew up in an active LDS home. It was also a very abusive home. I married a returned missionary in the temple when I was twenty years old. He also was abusive to me and to our children. I won't go into details, but I will say that for my whole life I have tried very hard to do what is right and to follow my Lord. After fasting and much prayer, I felt that I had the answer to leave the situation with my children. Less than a year later I met my present husband, who adopted the children and has treated us with kindness and respect.

"At the time you came to our conference, I was struggling very heavily with inner feelings—anger, resentment, and hurt—caused by the abuse I had suffered. I had been struggling and trying to heal from them for about ten years, and I was feeling like I was making no progress at all. I felt like a wicked, horrible person for even having such feelings, and I was depressed all the time and really struggled daily to just func-tion minimally. Words that I heard every week at church like mother, father, family, etc., were triggers to such dark emotions in me. I was having a hard time living with myself. In fact, every time I had contact with any member of my birth family, I fought the strongly compelling urge to drive up in the moun-tains and put a bullet in my head. It was truly a horrible time for me.

"When I heard you were coming for the conference, I told my family I wasn't going to go. They had announced that the theme of the conference was families, and I knew I didn't want to sit there and become more and more depressed as everyone talked about a subject that caused me so much pain and dark-ness. I lay in bed that morning, listening to my family getting ready to go to church, feeling only bitterness that the confer-ence had to be about some subject that made it impossible for me to attend. Just twenty minutes before the conference started, I found myself on my feet and at my closet, looking for something to wear. I didn't remember getting out of bed, and I wondered why I was even getting ready to go. I don't think I've ever gotten ready to go anywhere that fast before or since, but when it was time to leave, I was ready.

"I sat there through the conference, wondering why I was there. I didn't want to be there. The talks really depressed me and made me feel like I didn't belong—just like I knew they would. I wanted to get up and leave, but for some reason I couldn't get out of my chair. Then you got up to speak, and at first, it was just more of the same. Then you paused for a moment. You apologized because of the sensitive nature of what you were about to say, but you said that you felt impressed to say it. I felt a jolt go through my body like an electrical shock. I knew what you were about to say was for me. And even though I never cry in public, the tears started pouring down my cheeks.

"You said, 'There is a woman sitting here in the congregation today who has suffered from abuse. Perhaps it was a neighbor or a friend, a brother or most horribly, a father.' You went on to say that it was time to let go of the hate and bitterness and to apply the atoning blood of Christ to heal the wounds, and that through fasting and prayer I could let go of the sorrow of the past. Then you went on and finished the talk you had started.

"I knew I needed to talk with you afterward, and my good friend encouraged me and even went up with me. There was a long line of people that day because of the change in the stake presidency, and though I am easily discouraged by such things (and was even more so back then), we waited and went through the line. When I got to you and shook your hand, I said, 'You were talking to me.' You just looked me in the eyes for a moment and then I knew you understood what I was trying to say to you. I will never forget how you said, 'I'm so sorry. Can you let go of it?' I told you that I didn't know. I was trying, but I just hadn't been able to do it. You told me to read Moroni 7. You told me several times to read that chapter. Then I thanked you and left.

"I did read Moroni 7. It became my own personal scripture for a long time. I pored over it like I had never pored over another scripture in my life. I prayed so fervently. I felt strongly that I needed to make a break from my family, so I cut all communication with them. For several years before that, I had only had minimal contact with them. But I felt that in order to heal, I needed no contact at all. So I wrote a letter to my parents, and for over three years there was no contact there. I know it hurt my parents, and I was sure my brothers and sisters would not understand. But I felt like I was doing what I needed to do for me. More important, I felt like I was doing what my Father in Heaven wanted me to do.

"In time, I did feel myself healing as my relationship with my Savior deepened and strengthened. I grew to love Him so very much and to trust in Him. Finally, my children desired to have contact with my family again. I wasn't sure it was right and so I prayed about it. I prayed for eight months because I didn't want to get back into the family only to find I couldn't handle the feelings that would crop up. It seemed the more I prayed about it, the worse I felt, until those last two months were a living hell. I felt so dark and such anger and rage and bitterness—more than I had felt in several years. One night I couldn't sleep. It was one of many nights that sleep eluded me during those months. I lay there in my bed praying for about two hours. Finally, I said amen and just lay there listening.

"A voice in my mind started asking me questions, and I thought very hard before I answered each one. When the last one was answered, I understood a lot better why I was having such a hard time letting go of the anger. I was thinking about this when suddenly all the darkness, anger, and bitterness were sucked out of my body. It was a physical sensation as well as an emotional feeling. I was afraid to move. I was afraid that if I did move, the dark stuff would be sucked back in, and I didn't want that. I lay there for perhaps a minute, when suddenly I was filled with the most incredible feeling of love. It took the place of where the dark feelings had been. I could hardly wait for morning to come so I could call my parents. When I did, we were all crying.

"In the time since that reunion, I have never had any of those ugly feelings return. I found that while I was healing, so were my family members. I have seen some pretty miraculous things in my life. I had a blessing once from a prophet that healed my body of a terminal illness, but the miracle I received in being able to forgive my family and love them again is the most incredible and miraculous thing I've ever witnessed in my life. I could not do it on my own. I tried for many years. When the healing came, it was a gift, freely and lovingly given."

This wonderful sister, though she had suffered for many years, approached the pinnacle of the Savior's Sermon on the Mount. The pursuit of godliness begins with the realization that we are poor in spirit and need to come unto Him to be healed. We then mourn for our sins with a broken heart and a contrite spirit. Next, we hunger and thirst after righteousness until we are filled with the Holy Ghost. As we extend mercy to others, we are blessed by His mercy. As we expunge feelings of vengeance from our mind and soul, we become pure in heart. We wish to extend His peace to others, and we are able to love our enemies and pray for those who curse us, hate us, or spitefully abuse or persecute us (3 Nephi 12:3–12; Matthew 5:43–44).

President Gordon B. Hinckley observed: "Most of us have not reached that stage of compassion and love and forgiveness. It is not easy. It requires a self-discipline almost greater than we are capable of. But as we try, we come to know that there is a resource of healing, that there is a mighty power of healing in Christ, and that if we are to be His true servants we must not only exercise that healing power in behalf of others, but, perhaps more important, inwardly.

"I would that the healing power of Christ might spread over the earth and be diffused through our society and into our homes, that it might cure men's hearts of the evil and adverse elements of greed and hate and conflict. I believe it could happen. It believe it must happen. If the lamb is to lie down with the lion, then peace must overcome conflict, healing must mend injury."[6]

President Hinckley has added, "If the world is to be

improved, the process of love must make a change in the hearts of mankind. It can do so when we look beyond self to give our love to God and others, and do so with all our heart, with all our soul, and with all our mind."[7]

The miracle of extending and receiving forgiveness is the greatest miracle of all and the emulation of divine love.

NOTES

1. As told to and recorded by Elder David Nelson.

2. Smith, *Gospel Doctrine*, 435–36.

3. Smith, *Doctrines of Salvation*, 1:196.

4. McConkie, *Angels*, 89–90.

5. Maxwell, "Notwithstanding My Weakness," *Ensign*, November 1976, 14.

6. Hinckley, "The Healing Power of Christ," *Ensign*, November 1988, 59.

7. Hinckley, *Faith—The Essence of True Religion*, 49.

EIGHTEEN

Ether's Song of Faith

Wherefore, whoso believeth in God might with surety hope for a better world, yea, even a place at the right hand of God, which hope cometh of faith, maketh an anchor to the souls of men, which would make them sure and steadfast, always abounding in good works, being led to glorify God (Ether 12:4).

The Savior, during His visit to the ancient Nephites, and the prophet Ether are the only ones in the Book of Mormon to refer to the building of the New Jerusalem. Like his prophetic predecessors, Ether testified with great faith and certainty, not only of the "days of Christ" (Ether 13:4), which lay hundreds of years in the future, but also of the building of the New Jerusalem, which was to occur more than two thousand years beyond the "days of Christ" on earth. Such testimony and prophetic insight come from the power of faith and the power of the Spirit. These powers can confirm future events with such strong assurance that they become undeniable, allowing prophets to refer to them in the past tense even though they have not yet occurred (2 Nephi 25:26; Jarom 1:11; Mosiah 3:13; Mosiah 16:6).

Moroni described Ether as a mighty "prophet of the Lord;

wherefore Ether came forth in the days of Coriantumr, and began to prophesy unto the people, for he could not be restrained because of the Spirit of the Lord which was in him. For he did cry from the morning, even until the going down of the sun, exhorting the people to believe in God unto repentance lest they should be destroyed, saying unto them that by faith all things are fulfilled" (Ether 12:2–3).

THE GIFTS OF THE SPIRIT

In this dispensation, President Brigham Young promised the Saints: "If a person lives according to the revelations given to God's people, he may have the Spirit of the Lord to signify to him his will, and to guide and to direct him in the discharge of his duties, in his temporal as well as his spiritual exercises. I am satisfied, however, that in this respect, *we live far beneath our privileges*" with the Spirit.[1]

During His earthly ministry, the Savior often referred to various gifts of the Spirit. These gifts include the knowledge that Jesus Christ is the Son of God, the ability to believe the testimonies of others, the gifts of wisdom and knowledge, the gift of tongues, the faith to heal and be healed, and the power to work miracles, prophesy, and discern spirits (1 Corinthians 12:3–11; Moroni 10:8–18; D&C 46: 8–29). When we live close to the Spirit, we reap the fruit of the Spirit, which includes "love, joy, peace, longsuffering, gentleness, goodness, faith, meekness, [and] temperance" (Galatians 5:22–23).

QUALIFYING FOR THE SPIRIT

Given such a comforting catalogue of privileges with the Spirit, it is almost inconceivable that we would choose to live beneath our privileges. One of the most obvious reasons for doing so is our failure to qualify for the companionship of the Spirit. Contention, profanity, pornography, raucous music, selfishness, greed, and a host of other offenses cause the Spirit to withdraw from us or cause us to withdraw from the Spirit (Mosiah 2:36).

More than a year before the restored Church was officially organized, the Lord revealed to the Prophet Joseph Smith the prerequisites for working in the Kingdom: "And faith, hope, charity and love, *with an eye single to the glory of God,* qualify him for the work" (D&C 4:5; emphasis added). Our frequent failure to focus—with an eye single to the glory of God—upon the things of eternity is another reason we fail to qualify for the Spirit. It is rather difficult while watching television to receive inspiration for our next gospel doctrine lesson. It is also impossible to receive inspiration and guidance concerning our children's welfare while we are in the midst of contention. James observed, "A double minded man is unstable in all his ways" (James 1:8).

One possible reason we experience discouragement in a Church calling is that we seek to do the Lord's work in our own way rather than in His way. It is significant that the early fishermen called to be Jesus' disciples "straightway left their nets, and followed him" (Matthew 4:20). They were no longer to be fishermen but rather "fishers of men" (Matthew 4:19), and this required a change of focus—indeed, an eye single to the glory of God. Our spiritual progress will increase when we no longer drag our progress-impeding nets behind us, such as our bad habits, doubts, fears, and failure to focus on the things that matter most eternally.

King Benjamin posed a profound soul-searching question: "For how knoweth a man the master whom he has not served, and who is a stranger unto him, and is far from the thoughts and intents of his heart?" (Mosiah 5:13). We can hardly qualify for spiritual promptings to do right when the thoughts and intents of our hearts lean in the opposite direction. On the

other hand, we can claim the Lord's promise that "if ye are purified and cleansed from all sin, ye shall ask whatsoever you will
in the name of Jesus and it shall be done" (D&C 50:29).

ASKING FOR THE SPIRIT

The invitation to claim the privileges of the Spirit is open
to all. However, for many reasons we often simply fail to ask
our Father in Heaven to send His Spirit to assist us in making
decisions and resolving life's perplexities. One reason the
Prophet Joseph Smith was selected to be the Lord's instrument
in restoring the gospel and priesthood keys was that he *asked*
for further light and knowledge, putting James' promise to the
test: "If any of you lack wisdom, let him ask of God" (James
1:5).

Many of the revelations contained in the Doctrine and
Covenants were an outgrowth of the Prophet's personal searching. As he would approach the very edge of his knowledge, he
would turn to a higher source of enlightenment and divine
direction. The Lord's promise to Joseph is a promise that we too
may claim: "If thou shalt ask, thou shalt receive revelation upon
revelation, knowledge upon knowledge, that thou mayest
know the mysteries and peaceable things—that which bringeth
joy, that which bringeth life eternal" (D&C 42:61).

EXPERIENCE

Experience in our church callings gives us a sense of grow-
ing competence and self-confidence, but in our comfort lies a
caveat. With the passage of weekly and monthly meetings, our
problem-solving repertoire increases, and as months merge into
years, our experience can cause us to resolve each new challenge the same way we solved similar problems in the past. If
we are not careful, experience may exclude the Spirit from our
lives. Not every family welfare problem can be solved with the

same approach. Not every child should be disciplined the way siblings were disciplined. Not every congregation will be inspired by the same sermon given previously in another setting.

We would do well to remind ourselves of the method the Savior used in calling His apostles. As the Lord was walking along the seacoast, he climbed aboard Simon Peter's little boat, which was docked at the beach. He asked Peter to row a short distance from the shore, and while seated in the boat, the Savior began to teach the people. At the conclusion of His instruction, He gently commanded Peter, "Launch out into the deep, and let down your nets for a draught." Peter mildly protested, "Master, we have toiled all the night, and have taken nothing: *nevertheless,* at thy word I will let down the net" (Luke 5:4–5; emphasis added).

Nevertheless is an extremely important word throughout the scriptures. In the depths of His agony in the Garden of Gethsemane, the Savior prayed, "Nevertheless not my will, but thine, be done" (Luke 22:42). In the first section of the Doctrine and Covenants, the Lord declared, "For I the Lord cannot look upon sin with the least degree of allowance; nevertheless, he that repents and does the commandments of the Lord shall be forgiven" (D&C 1:31–32). But for the word "nevertheless" in the respective contexts of these two passages, our sojourn on this mortal sphere would be hopeless. Notwithstanding the agony that caused the Savior to bleed from every pore, He did not abrogate His atoning sacrifice. And notwithstanding that each of our lives is pockmarked with countless craters of sin, precisely because of the Atonement, we can be forgiven when we repent.

Peter was hesitant to launch into the deep after spending a long night catching no fish. Nevertheless, he followed the Savior's command. As a result, Peter and his fishing partners caught so many fish that their nets began to break and their boats began to sink. "When Simon Peter saw it, he fell down at Jesus' knees, saying, Depart from me; for I am a sinful man, O Lord" (Luke 5:8). Jesus knew that Peter was a sinful man, just as He knows that each of us is sinful, but the Savior gave him a test, which he passed. Elder Neal A. Maxwell has observed that "God does not begin by asking us about our ability, but only about our availability, and if we then prove our dependability, he will increase our capability!"[2]

Because Peter willingly launched his boat out to sea, even though fishing had been unsuccessful that day, he proved to the Lord that he was willing to obey. So the Savior extended a call to Peter and his brother, Andrew: "Follow me, and I will make you fishers of men" (Matthew 4:19). Generally speaking, the wisdom of the business world would argue that if Jesus were trying to identify executive potential in someone who could in three years' time serve as the CEO or chief apostle of the primitive Church, He would look to the council of the Sanhedrin or to successful merchants whose leadership abilities were proven. But the Savior started with fishermen whose previous learning would not stand in the way of inspired instruction, and who would not become defensive or cave in when chastened and corrected. Nor did those simple fishermen have competing interests crowding out time needed to serve the Lord. As with young Joseph Smith, the early apostles' lack of knowledge and experience ensured that they would have humble hearts, listening ears, and open minds.

TRADITION

An extension of experience is tradition. The Prophet Joseph Smith shared a painful observation: "I have tried for a number of years to get the minds of the Saints prepared to receive the things of God; but we frequently see some of them . . . fly to pieces like glass as soon as anything comes that is contrary to their traditions: they cannot stand the fire at all."[3]

Many family traditions and national customs instill in us lofty feelings of loyalty and patriotism. But some traditions can also stifle the workings of the Spirit. The recurrent reference to the wicked "traditions of their fathers" throughout the Book of Mormon is a case in point. Some of the descendants of Laman and Lemuel perpetuated wicked traditions throughout the centuries, causing their posterity to wander in unbelief.

Wards and stakes may develop wonderful traditions of performing excellent plays and musicals and of sponsoring competitive athletic events, interesting youth conferences, entertaining dances, and inspiring firesides. As vitally important as each of these traditional events may be, it is occasionally prudent to reassess such traditions in light of family and home. If we are not careful, a good and deeply ensconced tradition may subtly subvert the Spirit, which may seek to steer us in a different direction. We are grateful for living prophets and apostles, led by President Gordon B. Hinckley, whose sensitivity to the Spirit regarding temple building caused a dramatic departure from a well-established tradition of building a few large temples to building many smaller temples throughout the earth.

MISINTERPRETATION OF POLICIES

As important as handbooks, policies, and guidelines are, we must always be open to that rare exception to policy for justifiable reasons, and we must be sure that we understand the policy before making exceptions. The Savior's handling of the incident with the woman taken in the act of adultery did not demonstrate that He was soft on sin but rather that there was an alternative way of handling the situation short of stoning the sinner (John 8:2–11).

The apostle Paul warned the rule-following Saints in Corinth that "the letter killeth, but the spirit giveth life" (2 Corinthians 3:6), and President J. Reuben Clark Jr. cautioned us that "regimentation can stifle revelation."[4] In latter-day revelation the Lord has counseled us that "notwithstanding those things which are written, it always has been given to the elders of my church from the beginning, and ever shall be, to conduct all meetings as they are directed and guided by the Holy Spirit" (D&C 46:2). A departure from the printed program allowing a new convert to bear a testimony, or a variation in the schedule permitting an elderly faithful sister to share an inspiring experience, or spontaneously calling upon a recently activated brother to offer the benediction can all work to inspire hearts and bless lives. Planning and policies are extremely important, but listening to the Spirit is indispensable in performing the work of the Lord.

We gain some valuable insight from the Nephites with regard to adherence to policy. Five years before the Savior's birth, Samuel the Lamanite prophesied that "many signs and wonders in heaven" would signal to the inhabitants of ancient America that Jesus Christ had been born in the eastern hemisphere (Helaman 14:1–12). As soon as these signs appeared, some thought it "no more expedient to observe the law of Moses" (3 Nephi 1:24).

Amulek had summarized well the teachings of his prophetic predecessors, declaring, "This is the whole meaning of the law, every whit pointing to that great and last sacrifice; and that great and last sacrifice will be the Son of God, yea, infinite and eternal" (Alma 34:14). All of the feast days and fast days and rites and rituals practiced among the Israelites and their Nephite cousins directed the people's attention to the coming of the Messiah.

Thus, when the signs in heaven announced the Savior's

birth, it seemed perfectly logical for many of the Nephites to assume that the law of Moses had been fulfilled and they would no longer be required to abide by it. What they did not fully understand was that their blood sacrifices were a type and a shadow of the shedding of the blood of the Lamb of God. It was not His birth that fulfilled the law but rather His atoning sacrifice for sin. Some of the Nephites were thirty-three years premature in assuming they could abandon the law of Moses.

At the other end of the continuum, even after the Savior's voice had been heard to declare in the darkness that "in me is the law of Moses fulfilled" (3 Nephi 9:17), many "wondered what he would concerning the law of Moses; for they understood not the saying that old things had passed away" (3 Nephi 15:2). After Jesus personally appeared to the Nephites, he again testified to them, "I have come to fulfil the law; therefore it hath an end" (3 Nephi 15:5).

We can derive great wisdom, power, and strength from following the counsel of our living apostles and prophets. We must neither lead them nor impede them.

FAMILY HISTORY

For many years the Genealogical Society of Utah sponsored the microfilming of important vital statistics and other information found in archives throughout many nations. The microfilms of these public records were then made accessible to members of the Church and the general public at the Church's more than 3,700 family history centers in 65 countries throughout the world. For many years an unwritten rule discouraged proselytizing among patrons of other faiths. It was assumed that because the records were obtained from the public domain, the general public should have access to them with no strings attached.

On May 16, 1997, President Boyd K. Packer, on behalf of

the Quorum of the Twelve, sent a letter to priesthood leaders titled "Expanding the Use of Family History Centers." Attached to this letter were guidelines "designed to help leaders make use of family history centers for missionary work without compromising the research purpose of these facilities." The response to this important letter has been interesting, amusing, and, for some directors and staff members within family history centers, mildly distressing. Much like the Nephites of old, some of them have overzealously emphasized missionary work, requiring patrons to receive one of the missionary discussions before they can get their hands on a microfiche reader. Others adamantly stifle any attempts at proselytizing, for that would, in their minds, compromise the research purposes of the facilities.

When we claim the privileges of the Spirit, we will know how to appropriately introduce the gospel to our friends, neighbors, and associates, including patrons of our family history centers. We will be able to explain in a nonthreatening way why we are so involved in family history research and thus awaken in them a greater interest in learning more about the gospel. Some family history staff members fear that a gospel discussion would discourage patrons from visiting our family history centers. There is no risk involved in gently introducing our family history patrons to the full-time missionaries and to the restored gospel of Jesus Christ. But to do so, we must be sensitive to the Spirit, and then the Spirit can become an important part of our efforts to share the gospel.

PRIDE

Inspiration and revelation come in different ways. One significant avenue of inspiration is the principle of presidencies and councils, by which several individuals openly discuss a difficult challenge and then synergistically combine their best thinking and prayerfully arrive at a consensus that has the ratification of the Spirit (D&C 107:27–31). The observation in Proverbs is sound indeed: "Where no counsel is, the people fall: but in the multitude of counsellors there is safety" (Proverbs 11:14).

Unfortunately, some leaders, including parents, are too proud to seek the counsel of others, and they assume that their calling or position constitutes authorization to "go it alone." To the extent that leaders ignore the advice of counselors and members of councils, they live beneath their privileges with the Spirit.

The presidency principle often serves as a fruitful source of inspiration as three members of a presidency approach a problem or concern from their different backgrounds, three different perspectives, three different fountains of knowledge, and three different personalities. When the counseling resources are expanded in ward and stake councils, whose members are all qualified to receive inspiration, the likelihood of revelation increases. In a "multitude of counsellors there is safety." The involvement of a greater number of counselors generally increases the time it takes to reach a decision, but the additional effort is worth it.

INCREASING OUR SENSITIVITY TO THE SPIRIT

Certain actions will help us qualify for the constant companionship of the Holy Ghost and to be more sensitive to the enticings of the Spirit as we face some of life's largest decisions, including those regarding our life's work and our choice of an eternal companion.

1. Keep the Sabbath day holy

Through Moses, the Lord said, "Verily my sabbaths ye shall keep: for it is a sign between me and you throughout your generations; that ye may know that I am the Lord that doth sanctify you" (Exodus 31:13). How well we observe the holiness of this day signifies how much we love the Lord. At least one day a week we need to push back the world from our lives and remove the noise so that we may better listen to the still, small voice of the Spirit.

2. Pay an honest tithe

When our oldest daughter and her husband were sealed in the temple, I was interested to know what kind of counsel the person performing the sacred ordinance would give to this new couple. The man performing the sealing had ten children and fifty grandchildren. Certainly he was well qualified to provide excellent counsel and the key to a successful marriage. His counsel to them was surprisingly very brief: "Always remember to pay an honest tithing and your marriage will be happy."

I have reflected on that pithy counsel many times. Certainly a happy marriage is based upon unselfishness, kindness, compassion, and placing the needs of others above our own. A married couple that pays a full, honest tithe will, through the persistent practice of paying tithing, develop those desirable traits of unselfishness.

3. Search the scriptures

In the first chapter of the Book of Mormon, we read of a vision Lehi had of the Savior and the Twelve Apostles. In this vision he is given a book to read, and "as he read, he was filled with the Spirit of the Lord" (1 Nephi 1:12). That is an experience we may all have, but much of the time we read the scriptures as we would read a novel or biography. The scriptures are much more than great literature or a historical record. When we "feast upon the words of Christ," as Nephi admonished us to do, we truly can claim the promise that "the words of Christ will tell [us] all things what [we] should do" (2 Nephi 32:3). The scriptures will become our life script.

Often the answers we seek are not on the printed page of the scriptures we are reading but rather in the prompting of the Spirit we receive *while* we are reading.

4. Pray daily and listen for an answer

After returning home from her mission to Kobe, Japan, our daughter, Heidi, served as a Japanese tour guide at the South Rim of the Grand Canyon. One afternoon she had some time off, so she actually hiked down into the canyon.

Because she was planning to be gone for just a few hours, she took no flashlight and very little food and water. As the sun began to set, she realized she should probably turn back. It had been an extremely hot day, and she had not drunk enough water. She began to experience the symptoms of dehydration, with tingling of the skin and acute nausea. As the canyon suddenly became very dark, she knew she was in trouble as she realized that there was no moonlight and that the stars did not adequately light the trail. Heidi prayed to her Heavenly Father for guidance to find her way back to the trail and for the strength to get to the top.

As she prayed, she heard, as it were, a voice that said, "Heidi, you are too exhausted to make it to the top, and you will not be able to clearly see the trail. Lie down where you are, and I will protect you and help you find the trail in the morning." This she did. The next morning she hiked four hours in the burning Arizona sun, resting frequently in the sporadic shady spots she could find. Eventually, she met some hikers who had started down the trail earlier that morning. They gave her some water, and she was able to find the strength to reach the top. She did not get what she had prayed for, but she received what she needed.

We need to learn to pray and to listen, and not be like Naaman, with preconceived expectations of how our prayers should be answered.

5. Claim the blessings of fasting

The most profound promises that can accrue to us through fasting are found in Isaiah 58: "Is not this the fast that I have chosen? To loose the bands of wickedness, to undo the heavy burdens, and to let the oppressed go free, and that ye break every yoke?" (Isaiah 58:6). As we come to Him in our emptiness, He will bless us with the fulness of His love and the blessings of the fulness of the gospel.

Some among us have experienced various forms of abusive behavior at the hands of others. We can let these harmful and hurtful experiences scar our entire life, or we can claim the blessings promised by the Lord through Isaiah. As we fast and pray to the Lord, He will "undo the heavy burdens," "let the oppressed go free," and "break every yoke." I promise.

6. Partake of the sacrament worthily

Inherent in the sacred sacrament prayer is a prescription with a profound promise. When we take upon ourselves the name of Jesus Christ, always remember Him, and keep His commandments, His Spirit will always be with us.

As we cultivate the companionship of the Spirit in our lives and live up to the privileges of the Spirit, we can claim Ether's promised blessing to the faithful: "Wherefore, whoso believeth in God might with surety hope for a better world, yea, even a place at the right hand of God, which hope cometh of faith, maketh an anchor to the souls of men, which would make them sure and steadfast, always abounding in good works, being led to glorify God" (Ether 12:4).

NOTES

1. Young, *Discourses of Brigham Young,* 32; emphasis added.

2. Maxwell, "It's Service, Not Status, That Counts," *Ensign,* July 1975, 7.

3. Smith, *Teachings,* 331.

4. Clark, *First Presidency Memorandum of Suggestions,* 29 March 1940, 1–2, 4.

NINETEEN

Moroni's Song of Grace

Yea, come unto Christ, and be perfected in him, and deny yourselves of all ungodliness; and if ye shall deny yourselves of all ungodliness, and love God with all your might, mind and strength, then is his grace sufficient for you, that by his grace ye may be perfect in Christ; and if by the grace of God ye are perfect in Christ, ye can in nowise deny the power of God (Moroni 10:32).

The main purpose of the Book of Mormon, as its subtitle declares, is to serve as "Another Testament of Jesus Christ." In so doing, it clarifies a host of doctrines in the Old Testament and New Testament from which many "plain and most precious" parts and "many covenants of the Lord" have been removed or distorted over time (1 Nephi 13:26). Among the precious teachings to be restored is the doctrine of the plan of salvation and the proper place and purpose in that plan of the fall of Adam and Eve: "Adam fell that men might be; and men are, that they might have joy. And the Messiah cometh in the fulness of time, that he may redeem the children of men from the fall" (2 Nephi 2:25–26).

A heretical notion to emerge throughout the centuries was the supposed need for infants to be baptized to rid them of the "original sin" of Adam and Eve. Thanks be to God for the Book of Mormon, which exhorts us to teach "repentance and baptism unto those who are accountable and capable of committing sin" and tells us that "little children need no repentance, neither baptism," for "little children are alive in Christ" (Moroni 8:10–12; Mosiah 3:16, 21; 15:25).

Hundreds of Christian denominations bear different names, but the Savior Himself asked the ancient Nephites, "And how be it my church save it be called in my name? For if a church be called in Moses' name then it be Moses' church; or if it be called in the name of a man then it be the church of a man; but if it be called in my name then it is my church, if it so be that they are built upon my gospel" (3 Nephi 27:8).

Considerable controversy exists in Christendom over the identity of Jehovah, the God of the Old Testament. The Book of Mormon resolves the issue with the words of the resurrected Jesus Christ: "Behold, I am he that gave the law, and I am he who covenanted with my people Israel; therefore, the law in me is fulfilled, for I have come to fulfil the law; therefore it hath an end. . . . Behold, I am the law, and the light. Look unto me, and endure to the end, and ye shall live; for unto him that endureth to the end will I give eternal life" (3 Nephi 15:5, 9).

When the Savior asked John the Baptist to baptize Him in the river Jordan, John was initially hesitant until Jesus said, "Suffer it to be so now: for thus it becometh us to fulfil all righteousness" (Matthew 3:15). Only from the teachings of Nephi do we learn how the Savior fulfilled all righteousness by being baptized. Notwithstanding the fact that He was holy, He was baptized to demonstrate to us and to His Father that He would humble Himself in keeping all the commandments. He also showed the "straitness of the path, and the narrowness of the gate" and extended an invitation to all of us: "Follow thou me" (2 Nephi 31:4–12).

Yet another area of important clarification provided by the Book of Mormon is the description of Christ's suffering in Gethsemane. The translation in most major languages mirrors the translation found in the King James version of the Bible:

"And he was withdrawn from them about a stone's cast, and kneeled down, and prayed, saying, Father, if thou be willing, remove this cup from me: nevertheless not my will, but thine, be done. And there appeared an angel unto him from heaven, strengthening him. And being in an agony he prayed more earnestly: and his sweat was *as it were* great drops of blood falling down to the ground" (Luke 22:41–44; emphasis added).

Some Christians believe that the Savior sweat blood in a figurative sense only, but latter-day revelation confirms that He did, indeed, bleed from every pore. More than a century before His actual agony in the Garden of Gethsemane, King Benjamin prophesied, "And lo, he shall suffer temptations, and pain of body, hunger, thirst, and fatigue, even more than man can suffer, except it be unto death; for behold, *blood cometh from every pore,* so great shall be his anguish for the wickedness and the abominations of his people" (Mosiah 3:7; emphasis added).

In the Doctrine and Covenants, the Savior testified that the suffering associated with His atonement "caused myself, even God, the greatest of all, to tremble because of pain, and to *bleed at every pore,* and to suffer both body and spirit" (D&C 19:18).

The difference between sweat and blood is the difference between a great mortal humanitarian teacher under stress and the Only Begotten Son of God taking upon Himself the sins of the world. The difference between sweat and blood is the difference between paying the price to finish a marathon and paying the price to purchase our souls. As Paul taught the Corinthians, "Ye are not your own . . . for ye are bought with a price" (1 Corinthians 6:19–20).

We could produce an endless list of doctrinal questions, issues, and concerns that are resolved by the Book of Mormon, but for our current purposes we will conclude with a discussion of the relationship between faith and works and being saved by grace.

Some theologians have contended that James' declaration that "faith without works is dead" (James 2:17–26) is a sharp contradiction of Paul's teaching that "man is justified by faith without the deeds of the law" (Romans 3:28). Others maintain, however, that the writings of James and the writings of Paul reveal little, if any, difference in their views. Frederic W. Farrar, a prominent nineteenth century British theologian, contends that this controversy between the importance of faith and works "only furnishes an illustration of the ease with which a theory, resting on a narrow basis of fact, may be pushed into complete extravagance. . . . But it is quite common for the adherents of great thinkers to exaggerate their difference, and fail to catch their spirit."[1]

JAMES ON FAITH

In addition to writing his oft-quoted passage on the importance of works, James also wrote extensively of the importance of faith:

"But let him ask in faith, nothing wavering" (James 1:6).

"Hearken, my beloved brethren, hath not God chosen the poor of this world rich in faith, and heirs of the kingdom which he hath promised to them that love him?" (James 2:5).

"Seest thou how faith wrought with his works, and by works was faith made perfect?" (James 2:22).

PAUL ON WORKS

Complementing his writings on faith, the apostle Paul included the importance of good works in several of his epistles:

"And God is able to make all grace abound toward you; that ye, always having all sufficiency in all things, may abound in every good work" (2 Corinthians 9:8).

"For we are his workmanship, created in Christ Jesus unto good works" (Ephesians 2:10).

"That ye might walk worthy of the Lord unto all pleasing, being fruitful in every good work, and increasing in the knowledge of God" (Colossians 1:10).

"Comfort your hearts, and stablish you in every good word and work" (2 Thessalonians 2:17)

"That they do good, that they be rich in good works" (1 Timothy 6:18).

"That the man of God may be perfect, thoroughly furnished unto all good works" (2 Timothy 3:17).

"In all things shewing thyself a pattern of good works" (Titus 2:7).

"And whatsoever ye do in word or deed, do all in the name of the Lord Jesus, giving thanks to God and the Father by him. . . . And whatsoever ye do, do it heartily, as to the Lord, and not unto men" (Colossians 3:17, 23).

Paul counseled the Roman Saints to be engaged in certain specific good works, such as "serving the Lord," "continuing instant in prayer," and "distributing to the necessity of saints." He also counseled them to "bless, and curse not," "weep with them that weep," "be of the same mind one toward another," "provide things honest in the sight of all men," "live peaceably," "give [thine enemy] drink," and "overcome evil with good" (Romans 12:11–18, 20–21).

Paul taught both the Corinthians and the Galatians the law of the harvest—that they would reap what they sowed, not merely what they believed (2 Corinthians 9:6–7; Galatians 5:6). And he exhorted the Ephesians to become actively engaged in taking upon themselves "the whole armour of God" (Ephesians 6:13–18).

RESOLUTION

Author Stephen E. Robinson resolves the controversy over faith and works this way: "If we use Paul's definition of faith as faithfulness to the gospel covenant, then we find that Paul's formula in Romans 3:28 is correct: Faith alone (commitment to the gospel) *will* justify us to God, even without living the law of Moses. On the other hand, if we define faith as James does—as mere belief—then James' formula is also correct: Mere belief or affirmation without good behavior is insufficient by itself to justify us before God. . . . Both apostles teach the truth. Where we get into trouble is in combining James' definitions with Paul's formula or vice versa."[2]

Frederic W. Farrar, shared essentially the same observation regarding the differing definitions of Paul and James:

"For by *Faith* St. Paul never means dead faith (*fides informis*) at all. He means (1), in the lowest sense of the word, general trust in God (*assensus, fiducia*); then (2) self-surrender to God's will; in its highest and most Pauline sense—the sense in which he uses it when he speaks of "Justification by Faith"—it is self-surrender which has deepened into sanctification; it is a living power of good in every phase of life; it is *unio mystica,* a mystical incorporation with Christ in unity of love and life. But this application of the word was peculiar to St. Paul, and St. James does not adopt it. He meant by faith in *this* passage a mere theoretical belief—belief which may exist without any germinant life—belief which may stop short at a verbal profession of Jewish orthodoxy—belief which does not even go so far as that of demons—belief which, taken alone, is so inappreciable in value that he compares it to a charity which speaks words of idle comfort and does not give.

"Again, by *Works* the two writers meant very different things. St. Paul was thinking mainly of those works which stood high in the estimation of his Jewish opponents; he meant the works and observances of the Levitical and ceremonial Law—new moons, sabbaths, sacrifices, ablutions, meats, drinks, phylacteries, and so forth;—or, at the very highest, works of ordinary duty, 'deeds of the Law,' untouched by emotion, not springing from love to God. He did *not* mean, as St. James did, works of love and goodness done in obedience to the royal law, those works which spring from a true and lively faith, which *must* spring from it, which it is as impossible to sever from it as to sever from fire its light and heat. . . .

"Briefly, then, it may be said that the works which St. Paul thinks of are the works of the Law, those of St. James the works of godliness; that St. Paul speaks of deep and mystic faith, St. James of theoretic belief; that St. Paul has in view the initial justification of a sinner, St. James the complete justification of a believer."[3]

After discarding atheism for deism and then ultimately converting to Christianity, C. S. Lewis observed that "Christians have often disputed as to whether what leads the Christian home is good actions, or Faith in Christ. . . . It does seem to me like asking which blade in a pair of scissors is most necessary. A serious moral effort is the only thing that will bring you to the point where you throw up the sponge. Faith in Christ is the only thing to save you from despair at that point: and out of that Faith in Him good actions must inevitably come."[4]

Just as Jewish orthodoxy requires adherence to certain laws or commandments, so the Roman Catholic Church requires participation in certain sacraments, including baptism, confirmation, confession, anointing the sick, marriage, holy orders for those embarking on a clerical career, and the Eucharist, or holy communion. Many other Christian churches place greater emphasis upon being saved by faith or grace in lieu of participation in various sacraments or ordinances.

The question is often asked of Latter-day Saints: Do you believe in being saved by grace? Elder Bruce C. Hafen, Stephen E. Robinson, and others have pointed out that Latter-day Saints often retreat from this question. But Latter-day Saints know for certain that they must participate in certain exalting ordinances: being baptized, receiving the Holy Ghost, being ordained to the Melchizedek Priesthood (if male), receiving the temple endowment, and being sealed in the Holy Temple to a spouse for time and for all eternity. The gospel includes many other ordinances, such as the blessing of the sick and the blessing and naming of infants, the sacrament, patriarchal blessings, and ordinations to the offices of the Aaronic Priesthood. These, however, are not saving ordinances.

So where do we stand compared to other churches regarding grace? The Book of Mormon is replete with references to the grace of God and the fact that "redemption cometh in and through the Holy Messiah; for he is full of grace and truth" (2 Nephi 2:6; Alma 5:48; 9:26; 13:9; 2 Nephi 9:8; 10:24).

Nephi explained it best: "For we labor diligently to write, to persuade our children, and also our brethren, to believe in Christ, and to be reconciled to God; *for we know that it is by grace that we are saved, after all we can do*" (2 Nephi 25:23; emphasis added). What a marvelous reconciliation of the controversy between justification by faith and "faith without works is dead"! Paul and James are reconciled, and now our challenge is to become reconciled to Christ by accepting the loving invitation extended by the last prophet of the Book of Mormon:

"Yea, come unto Christ, and be perfected in him, and deny yourselves of *all* ungodliness; and if ye shall deny yourselves of *all* ungodliness, and love God with all your might, mind and strength, then is his *grace* sufficient for you, that by his *grace* ye may be perfect in Christ; and if by the *grace* of God ye are perfect in Christ, ye can in nowise deny the power of God.

"And again, if ye by the *grace of God* are perfect in Christ, and deny not his power, then are ye sanctified in Christ by the *grace of God* through the shedding of the blood of Christ, which is in the covenant of the Father unto the remission of your sins, that ye become holy, without spot" (Moroni 10:32–33; emphasis added).

We should not get caught up in a compulsive chronology of whether faith precedes our works or whether grace is applied after all we can do. The main lesson is that the invitation to come unto Christ is open to all, and that His grace will attend us throughout life's entire exam, not just after the scores have been recorded and the diplomas have been awarded.

CLEANSING POWER

Several years ago we had the blessing of accompanying President Gordon B. Hinckley and his wife, Sister Marjorie Hinckley, to a regional conference in Portugal. President Hinckley shared the following story, which I paraphrase:

"I have a friend who is an attorney in a large skyscraper in Los Angeles. A few years ago he had a secretary with a terrible addiction to tobacco. She was such a heavy smoker one could tell when she got off the elevator in the morning without looking at her. After twenty years of smoking she had a strong desire to quit, and one day she walked into my friend's office and said: 'I notice you don't smoke.' My friend responded, 'And I notice that you do.'

"Assuming that everyone had faced a smoking problem at one time or another, the secretary implored her employer: 'Is there anything you could recommend that would help me quit smoking?' My friend reached into his desk drawer and retrieved a book with a dark blue cover and golden lettering and handed it to his secretary with the directions: 'Read this, and then you'll quit smoking.' His secretary was effusive in her gratitude: 'Thank you,' she said with a note of desperation.

"The next morning, to my friend's surprise, his secretary stormed into his office obviously very agitated. 'You promised me that if I read that book I would quit smoking,' she began with a voice tinged in irritation. 'I stayed up half the night and read 170 pages, and there wasn't a single reference to smoking.' My friend replied simply, 'Continue reading the book.'

"The second morning his secretary was even more agitated than the day before. 'I have read 330 pages,' she proclaimed in a raised voice, 'and there has not been one single mention of cigarettes or tobacco.' My friend smiled and said, 'Read on.'

"The third morning she was fit to be tied. 'I have nearly completed the book,' she said. 'I have finished 500 pages, and there still has been no mention of tobacco or of smoking of any kind.' My friend benevolently prompted her to 'finish the book.'

"The fourth morning was different from the previous three mornings. She arrived quietly and somewhat subdued. She knocked gently on his office door and asked her boss if he might have a few minutes to talk. 'Of course,' he replied. Rather haltingly she started to explain what had happened the prior evening. 'I had a very unusual experience last night, and I'm not sure if I can really explain what happened, but I need to speak to someone about it. I finished the book as you encouraged me to do. Toward the end of the book, in the last chapter, I encountered a promise that if I would read the book and pray about it, I would know whether it is true.'

"'Well,' she continued, 'I had already lost three nights' sleep, so I thought I had nothing to lose by putting the promise to the test. I knelt down and began a simple prayer, and as I was on my knees a warm feeling started at the top of my head and proceeded throughout my body, and I felt as if I were being cleansed and purified. And this morning when I arose, for the first time in twenty years, I had completely lost a desire to smoke. Thank you, thank you, thank you.'"

President Hinckley concluded the story by saying, "I heard this story from her own lips as she was seated across the dining room table from me in the home of the president of the stake in which she was serving in the Relief Society presidency."

Such is the great cleansing power of the Book of Mormon and of the miracle of forgiveness. And such is a manifestation of the grace of God in conjunction with our own personal exertions in our life-long quest for perfection.

All apostles and prophets testify of Jesus Christ and His infinite atoning sacrifice, and each is a special witness of Christ and His divine mission. Each of them, in his own unique way, sings the song of redeeming love, a love captured in lyric by Isaac Watts.

> When I survey the wondrous cross
> On which the Prince of glory died,
> My richest gain I count but loss,
> And pour contempt on all my pride.
> Forbid it, Lord, that I should boast,
> Save in the death of Christ, my God!
> All the vain things that charm me most,
> I sacrifice them to his blood . . .
> Were the whole realm of nature mine,
> That were a present far too small;
> Love, so amazing, so divine,
> Demands my soul, my life, my all![5]

NOTES

1. Farrar, *Early Days of Christianity,* 351.

2. Robinson, *Following Christ,* 84.

3. Farrar, 356–57.

4. Lewis, *Mere Christianity,* 129.

5. Russell M. Nelson, "These . . . Were Our Exmples," *Ensign,* November 1991, 61.

Epilogue

One of the most profound messages of the Book of Mormon is that "men are, that they might have joy" (2 Nephi 2:25), and that joy is realized when we accept the Savior's urgent plea: "Will ye not now return unto me, and repent of your sins, and be converted, that I may heal you?" (3 Nephi 9:13).

We experience true joy only when we are willing to empty our lives of dross in order to make room for the fulness of the gospel.

C. S. Lewis contended that "There are only two kinds of people in the end: those who say to God, 'Thy will be done,' and those to whom God says, in the end, '*Thy* will be done.'"[1] Those who do the Father's will receive a celestial reward, and those who insist on their own will receive a lesser reward (D&C 76). King Lamoni's father demonstrated his desire to submit his will to the will of the Father when he prayed with the promise: "I will give away all my sins to know thee" (Alma 22:18). That is precisely what each of us must do if we are to know our Heavenly Father and His Son Jesus Christ and regain their presence.

Every prophet of the Book of Mormon speaks of hope and affirmation that a loving Father in Heaven patiently stands in the road, as it were, beckoning the return of each of His prodigal sons and daughters. From the lives of these prophets we gain glimpses of their own mortality and of their personal struggles to overcome dissension in the family, apostasy creeping into the flock, unbridled pride among their people, persecution from nonbelievers, and potentially paralyzing discouragement when the road ahead and seas to cross seem so daunting. But all of these prophets eventually claim victory over the world and over themselves, causing them to sing the song of redeeming love.

There are few better examples of scarlet sins becoming white as snow than the lives of Alma the younger and the four sons of Mosiah. Before their conversion they were described as "the very vilest of sinners," but once they had been granted forgiveness "they were desirous that salvation should be declared to every creature, for they could not bear that any human soul should perish" (Mosiah 28:4, 3).

Although these young men underwent great persecution and rejection during their missionary labors, they also experienced outstanding success as the Lord's instruments in converting the Lamanites in the lands of Ishmael, Middoni, Shilom, and Shemlon and the inhabitants of the cities of Nephi, Shimnilom and Lemuel (Alma 23:8–13). And these converts treated them "as though they were angels sent from God to save them from everlasting destruction" (Alma 27:4).

In Mormon's abridgement of the Nephite and Lamanite wars, he described Captain Moroni in the following superlative terms: "If all men had been, and were, and ever would be, like unto Moroni, behold, the very powers of hell would have been shaken forever; yea, the devil would never have power over the hearts of the children of men" (Alma 48:17). Mormon then compares Moroni to other men of great righteousness, declaring that Moroni "was a man like unto Ammon, the son of Mosiah, yea, and even the other sons of Mosiah, yea and also

Alma and his sons, for they were all men of God" (Alma 48:18). The atonement of Christ makes it possible for even the vilest of sinners to become men of God, but this transition requires a *mighty change* of heart, and the best time to begin making that change is now.

Whether one is a prison inmate, an excommunicated Church member, a victim of abuse, the injured party in an unsavory divorce or business deal gone sour, or the slave of an addictive habit, a loving Father sent His Son to earth to make things right and to lift and bless. He who bears scars from wounds in His hands, feet, and side knows how to heal all our wounds and remove all our scars.

When we accept the Savior's invitation to "come unto me," give away all our sins, and forgive others as we would be forgiven, we can claim His healing touch and reap His promise of lasting joy. It is then that we will sing the Song of Redeeming Love.

NOTE

1. Lewis, *The Great Divorce*, 72.

Additional Reading

LEHI

1 Nephi
10:2-6
2 Nephi
1:15
2:6–9, 25–28

NEPHI

1 Nephi
1:9, 20
10:4
11:13–33
15:13–15
19:9–10
21:13, 15–16
22:8–12
2 Nephi
4:20–35
11:4
19:6
25:13–17, 23–26
26:9, 24–25, 33
27:23
28:32
30:2, 5–8
31:13–21
33:6

ISAIAH

2 Nephi
21:10–12
22:1–6
Mosiah
14:2–12

JACOB

2 Nephi
6:11, 14, 17
8:3, 11
9:5–7, 10–13, 18–21, 25–26, 41
10:24–25
Jacob
1:7–8
4:4–5, 7–8, 11–12
6:4–5

ENOS

Enos
1:3–8, 27

KING BENJAMIN

Mosiah
3:5–12, 16–20
4:2–30
5:7–9

Sources

A Treasury of Christmas Songs and Carols. Edited by Henry W. Simon. Boston: Houghton Mifflin, 1955.

Bloxham, V. Ben, James R. Moss, and Larry C. Porter, ed. *Truth Will Prevail.* Salt Lake City: The Church of Jesus Christ of Latter-day Saints, 1987.

Browning, Elizabeth Barrett. *Aurora Leigh.* London: Smith, Elder, & Co., 1890.

Browning, Robert. *The Poetical Works of Robert Browning.* 2 vols. London: Smith, Elder & Co., 1902.

Chardin, Pierre Teilhard. *The Divine Milieu.* New York: Harper & Brothers, 1960

———. *The Future of Man.* New York: Harper and Row, 1964.

———. *The Phenomenon of Man.* New York: Harper and Row, 1959.

———. *Toward the Future.* New York: Harcourt Brace Jovanovich, 1975.

Conference Reports of The Church of Jesus Christ of Latter-day Saints. Salt Lake City: The Church of Jesus Christ of Latter-day Saints, 1898–.

Cowley, Matthias F. *Wilford Woodruff: History of His Life and Labors.* Salt Lake City: Bookcraft, 1964.

Farrar, Frederic W. *The Early Days of Christianity.* London: Cassell and Company, 1898.

Hafen, Bruce C. *The Broken Heart: Applying the Atonement to Life's Experiences.* Salt Lake City: Deseret Book, 1989.

Hinckley, Gordon B. *Faith—The Essence of True Religion.* Salt Lake City: Deseret Book, 1989.

Kierkegaard, Søren. *Concluding Unscientific Postscript.* Translated by David F. Swenson and Walter Lowrie. Princeton: Princeton University Press, 1941.

——. *Fear and Trembling.* Edited and translated by Howard V. Hong and Edna H. Hong. Princeton: Princeton University Press, 1983.

——. *The Sickness unto Death: A Christian Psychological Exposition for Upbuilding and Awakening.* Edited and translated by Howard V. Hong and Edna H. Hong. Princeton: Princeton University Press, 1980.

Kimball, Stanley B. *Heber C. Kimball, Mormon Patriarch and Pioneer.* Illinois: University of Illinois Press, 1981.

The Latter-day Saints' Millennial Star. Liverpool, England, 1840–70.

Lewis, C. S. *Mere Christianity,* New York: Macmillan, 1952.

——. *The Great Divorce.* New York: Macmillan, 1946.

——. *The Weight of Glory.* New York: Macmillan, 1980.

Madsen, Truman. *The Highest in Us.* Salt Lake City: Bookcraft, 1978.

McConkie, Oscar W., Jr. *Angels.* Salt Lake City: Deseret Book, 1975.

Oaks, Dallin H. "Revelation." In *Brigham Young University 1981–82 Fireside and Devotional Speeches.* Provo, Utah: Brigham Young University Publications, 1982.

Packer, Boyd K. *That All May Be Edified.* Salt Lake City: Bookcraft, 1982.

The Reader's Digest Merry Christmas Songbook. Edited by William L. Simon. Pleasantville, New York: Reader's Digest, 1981.

Robinson, Stephen E. *Following Christ.* Salt Lake City: Deseret Book, 1995.

Romney, Marion G. *The Price of Peace.* Brigham Young University Speeches of the Year, Provo, Utah, 1 March 1955.

Smith, Joseph. *History of The Church of Jesus Christ of Latter-day Saints.* Edited by B. H. Roberts. 2d ed. 7 vols. Salt Lake City: The Church of Jesus Christ of Latter-day Saints, 1932–51.

——. *Teachings of the Prophet Joseph Smith.* Selected by Joseph Fielding Smith. Salt Lake City: Deseret Book, 1976.

Smith, Joseph F. *Gospel Doctrine: Selections from the Sermons and Writings of Joseph F. Smith.* Salt Lake City: Deseret Book, 1971.

Smith, Joseph Fielding. *Doctrines of Salvation.* Compiled by Bruce R. McConkie. 3 vols. Salt Lake City: Bookcraft, 1954–56.

——. *The Way to Perfection.* Salt Lake City: Deseret Book, 1975.

Snow, Eliza R. *Biography and Family Record of Lorenzo Snow.* Salt Lake City: Deseret News, 1884.

Talmage, James. *Jesus the Christ.* Salt Lake City: Deseret Book, 1983.

Young, Brigham. *Discourses of Brigham Young.* Salt Lake City: Deseret Book, 1979.

Zweig, Stefan. *The Tide of Fortune: Twelve Historical Miniatures.* London: Cassell and Company, 1940.

Index

245